Just Within the Law

Juliet Pannett.
1974

Just Within the Law

HENRY CECIL

HUTCHINSON OF LONDON

Hutchinson & Co (Publishers) Ltd
3 Fitzroy Square, London W1

London Melbourne Sydney Auckland
Wellington Johannesburg Cape Town
and agencies throughout the world

First published 1975
© Henry Cecil 1975

Set in Monotype Baskerville
Printed in Great Britain by The Anchor Press Ltd
and bound by Wm Brendon & Son Ltd
both of Tiptree, Essex

ISBN 0 09 123070 5

⊞ Contents

⊞ On the Way to the Bar

A friend of mine, the late County Court judge, Basil Blagden, told me that, when he was a judge in India, he tried a case where it was necessary for a witness to prove his exact age, there being no birth certificate available. The witness swore that he was born on a particular date. The following dialogue ensued:

THE JUDGE: But you cannot know that yourself.
THE WITNESS: Yes, my Lord, I do.
THE JUDGE: You're not telling me that you can actually remember being born?
THE WITNESS: Yes, my Lord, I am.
THE JUDGE: Did it hurt?
THE WITNESS: Not particularly.

But the difficulty of remembering events of one's earliest childhood is only an incidental reason for my not referring to them. Another is because I do not believe that, except in the case of famous men, the average reader is interested in such details, but the main reason for my not mentioning them is that they would not be material to my object in writing this book.

For eighteen of my first fifty years in the law, that is to say, from 1949 to 1967, I led a double life. I was a judge and an author. What I have tried to do is to recount as accurately as possible events in my life which have some relationship to the two professions which I have been lucky enough to have been allowed to follow. Though, when I use the word 'accurately',

I have to remember what the late Mr Justice Macnaghten used to say about independent witnesses in accident cases. 'The courts,' he said, 'are full of honest witnesses, whose memories as the years go by become more and more certain and less and less accurate.'

I have nevertheless tried to recall how I came to start my two careers, how I progressed in each of them, some of the lessons which I may have learned, what I remember of some of the people with whom I came into contact and of some of the cases in which I was involved and where it has all led up till now. I have also mentioned my views about certain events and people and about our legal system, recognizing that others, better qualified to express an opinion on these subjects, may disagree with them. From all this the reader may get some idea of the sort of person I am, but I should make it plain that I am not intending to make any startling revelations or, except occasionally, to refer to events in my life which are wholly irrelevant to my two careers.

*

My decision to go to the Bar was made when I was fourteen. My eldest brother Edward, who was twenty-one at the time, was killed in the first war. He had been going to the Bar and after his death my parents asked me whether I would like to go instead. I had no idea of what going to the Bar entailed. We were not a legal family and we had no very close friends in the law. I just said yes. No pressure whatever was put on me by my parents, who would have been very happy for me to follow any lawful occupation. I do not remember why my eldest brother wanted to go to the Bar, but I have never regretted my choice, possibly because the Bar, as far as I can judge, is the most friendly of all the professions.

Even in the days when briefs were hard to come by and competition was therefore more fierce than it is today, when briefs are plentiful and barristers few in comparison, the relationship between members of the Bar was almost without exception of the happiest kind. It is impossible to speak with authority about any occupation which one has not in fact pursued, but I doubt if there is any profession where there is so little backbiting or jealousy and so much generosity as at the Bar. Naturally every barrister seeks to win a case in which he is engaged, but with trifling exceptions he never seeks to do this by using unfair methods. The more experienced advocate will often help his younger opponent. More than once litigants in a case have been surprised, and sometimes angered, on seeing the barristers representing them going off to lunch arm in arm.

In 1920 when I was eighteen I joined Gray's Inn and went to King's College, Cambridge. Of the four Inns of Court, the Inner Temple, the Middle Temple, Lincoln's Inn and Gray's Inn, Gray's Inn is the smallest. I joined it for the very simple reason that it was the cheapest. My parents were not at all well off and I have always found it difficult to understand how they managed to send three sons to a public school and then to a university. They had to be exceptionally economical and my mother kept detailed accounts of everything that was spent. We were an extremely happy family, but as a boy and very young man I unfairly resented the thrift which obtained in our household, although it was essential to our existence. Consequently, later on, when I had the opportunity, I was unreasonably extravagant.

I should have gone to Gray's Inn anyway for reasons of economy, but my father's other reasons for sending me there were because Lord Birkenhead was a member and because, my father said, owing to its size it was probably easier to become a Bencher there than at the other Inns.

Neither of us could have known at the time that I would become a County Court judge and that County Court judges (now called Circuit judges) are practically never made Benchers after their appointment. Although this well-known fact has in the past caused a certain amount of resentment among County Court judges, there is a good reason for it. Appointment as a Bencher is not a sinecure. A Bencher has many duties to perform and these duties have almost entirely to be performed in London. Judges of County Courts do their judicial work all over the country and it would be physically impossible for a judge in the country to be in London sufficiently often to discharge his duties as a Bencher. High Court judges, if not already Benchers on their appointment, are automatically made Benchers when they are made judges. This would be impossible in the case of County Court judges, unless they were appointed to London courts. If there were a rule that only judges appointed to the London courts were made Benchers, some new judges might ask to be appointed to a London court, and having been appointed, might later on ask to be transferred to the country. This would obviously be unsatisfactory. There is, moreover, a limit to the number of Benchers which an Inn can accommodate physically. It is indeed lucky for the Inns that Circuit judges are not automatically made Benchers on their appointment. The situation today would be completely intolerable. When I was appointed there were between fifty and sixty County Court judges. Today the number is over two hundred and fifty.

Lord Birkenhead had a big reputation in his day but he was not a great lawyer. There was, however, one great lawyer who was a Gray's Inn man, though at the time my father and I were wholly unaware of this. This was Lord Atkin, who was one of the greatest Common Lawyers Britain has ever produced, and probably the greatest of this century.

Most barristers quite rightly think that their own Inn is the best. For Gray's Inn I claim that it is the friendliest of all the Inns and that more notice is taken of the students by the Benchers than at the other Inns. I very much hope, however, that this fact will be disputed by members of the other Inns and that all the Benchers of all the Inns will compete for the reputation of doing most for the students.

For about 150 years after 1700 students had to take no examinations in order to be called to the Bar and the way in which they learned their law was by association with judges and barristers in the Inns of Court and in court itself. During those 150 years judges were appointed entirely from the Bar and the standard of judge was quite as high as it has been since then.

A Bar student starts his career by eating dinners at his Inn. Today some students complain at having to come long distances to eat a not very satisfactory meal and getting practically nothing else out of it. If the same attention were paid by Benchers and barristers to students as was paid between the years 1700 and 1850 there would certainly be no ground for this complaint.

Of course, some attention is paid to students. For example, three times in every two years each Inn of Court is allowed to occupy Cumberland Lodge in Windsor Great Park for a week-end. During this week-end there is full and free association between the Bar, the Bench and the students, while there are formal and informal talks and exercises and a very happy relationship is formed between those who are present. Unfortunately only a limited number can be there and three visits in two years are wholly insufficient.

In spite of these criticisms it is fair to say that much more is done for students today than in my day. During the whole of my three years as a student in Gray's Inn I do not recollect associating with anyone other than students. But I enjoyed it all very much indeed. In the first place I found it exciting to start my legal career when I was only eighteen and had only just become an undergraduate at Cambridge. Then the friendly atmosphere, the old traditions (such as drinking a toast out of a loving cup to the 'pious, glorious and immortal memory of Good Queen Bess') and the novelty of the new profession made me look forward to the dinners, particularly as they enabled me to have a week-end in London where we lived. I also found that my enthusiasm for the dinners was shared by friends of mine who did not live in London.

For each dinner I had to pay 3s 6d. We dined in messes of four and each mess was allotted a bottle of wine and a bottle of port, the charge for which was included in the 3s 6d. My taste for claret stems from my first dinner at Gray's Inn. My father knew quite a lot about wine, while I knew nothing. But I made a note of the name of the bottle of claret which we drank at my first dinner. It was Château Lafite 1899. When I told my father, he asked me to enquire whether it was too late for him to become a student. If the same standard of wine for students had been maintained up to today they would now be drinking Château Lafite 1953 instead of plonk. Hitler must answer for this decline.

*

I read classics in my first year at King's and law in my second and third years. There was no law don at my college and we had to go outside for tuition. Dr Frank Carr was my tutor. We thought he looked rather like a Roman horse and he had a very curious voice. He pronounced 'says' as 'sayze'. I shall always remember him saying 'Kewk sayze'. Quc was a French commentator on Roman law, but what he said and how his odd surname originated I haven't the faintest recollection.

Dr Carr's voice would not have mattered if the law which he imparted to us had been more accurate. I was told that he was a good teacher of Roman law, but I didn't take sufficient interest in it to be able to judge. That subject has at last been removed from the Bar examinations. Except in so far as any exercise for the mind is of some value to a student, and except for prospective Scots lawyers, it was a pretty good waste of time to have to learn it, particularly for those who had not read classics and for whom the Latin made things more difficult. But Roman law is the basis for much of Scots law.

One of the pieces of law which I remember Dr Carr teaching me was that one difference between the wrong known as a breach of contract and the wrong known as a tort, was that, while if you suffered no actual damage you could none the less get nominal damages for a tort, you could not get even nominal damages for a breach of contract unless you had suffered actual damage. This was an easy distinction for a student to learn and that is one of the reasons no doubt why I have always remembered it. Unfortunately it just happens to be wrong. You *can* get nominal damages for a breach of contract.

However, although it may be of some advantage to learn at

the university what the law is rather than what it isn't, it does not make all that difference, unless you are going in for an academic career. For the purpose of practice at the Bar it is the application of the law to facts that matters and you will only learn how to apply the law from actual practice. It was only after I had been practising for a few years and started to share a room with Frank Gahan, probably one of the finest lawyers never to have been made a judge, that I really began to learn any law.

Although we had no law don at King's we did have a law society and on one occasion a member of the then Court of Appeal came down to address us. He was Lord Justice Bankes and I have always remembered the advice which he gave us. He told us that he realized that we could not all expect to get Firsts in our examinations, but, he added, if we couldn't do that, it would be a considerable help to us if we could achieve distinction in the field of sport. For example, he told us, he had found it very useful personally to have become a rowing blue. By the time I received this advice I knew that I should not do enough work to achieve distinction in any examination and that, although there was nothing I should have liked better than to have obtained a rugger or a tennis blue, my career in both these fields was enthusiastic rather than successful. But, oddly enough, I was not discouraged.

Later on, when I encountered Lord Justice Bankes in the Court of Appeal and read some of his judgments in the Law Reports, I was not altogether surprised at what he had said to us. He was courteous on the Bench, but he lacked imagination and was no great lawyer. However, as he usually sat with two outstanding lawyers, he did little harm to English law. He was in fact senior to both of them and presided in a Court of Appeal (Bankes, Scrutton and Atkin L.JJ.) which, in spite of his presidency, was one of the most renowned in this century.

I'm afraid I didn't do much law when I was at Cambridge, although once I nearly came into conflict with it. In my second year I started to edit an undergraduate magazine called *The New Cambridge*. Our superior rival was *The Granta*, which survived till recently, but *The New Cambridge* died long ago. *The Granta* had run some sort of rag and, not unnaturally, we wanted to do something in return. We decided to make a film in the streets of Cambridge. It was to be a parody of a Wild West story. We called it *Red Beaver*, a name taken from a then popular and infantile game of beard-spotting which undergraduates used to play.

The most popular place and moment for a rag was King's Parade at noon on Saturday. We accordingly arranged for a scene to be taken of the villain tying up the heroine to a lamp-post on King's Parade at twelve noon on the following Saturday. On our placards we put 'Wanted – a crowd'. Within a very short time of the appearance of the placard a police inspector called on me and said that, unless I withdrew the placard, I would be charged with inciting a crowd to assemble for an unlawful purpose. I went at once to see Dr Carr, who told me that in his view the making of a parody of a Western film was not an unlawful purpose, even though made in the streets. As the streets are meant to enable people and vehicles to pass and repass and as a crowd would evidently prevent them from doing so, I am not sure that Dr Carr's opinion was any sounder than his view on damages for breach of contract, but fortunately its soundness did not have to be tested. Armed with his advice, I went straight to the police station and sought an interview with the police inspector. I told him that I had been advised that the purpose was not unlawful and that we proposed to continue to ask for a crowd.

A day or two later I received a summons from the senior proctor, the Reverend E. C. Hoskyns. This, of course, was a different matter. It would be no good quoting law to a senior proctor. I went to see him and he asked me what it was all about. I told him that *The Granta* had carried out what we thought was a not very successful rag and we wanted to do a better one. He said he quite understood that but why choose the busiest place on the busiest day at the busiest time? I said that that was the whole point. He replied that it might cause a good deal of inconvenience to the members of the community who had no connection with the university. I said that I thought some of them would be interested or amused at our antics but I agreed that some might be aggrieved.

'But it won't be for very long,' I said.

'How long?' he asked.

His question gave me an idea. 'If I will undertake to have the crowds off King's Parade', I asked him, 'by, say, 12.45, will you agree to our carrying on?'

He thought for a moment or two and then said: 'All right. If you'll give me your word, you can do it and I hope you'll enjoy it.'

I thanked him very much, and went straight to the police station. There I saw the police inspector and told him that I now had permission from the senior proctor to carry on. I also told him that I had promised to have the crowds off King's Parade by 12.45. I added that, unless the police would help me to do this, I might have great difficulty in keeping my word. The inspector said that he would certainly help. He asked me how many police I thought I would need and I told him that he would know better than I did. All I wanted was to be sure that at 12.40 – I deducted a precautionary five minutes – King's Parade would be clear of the crowd.

'Will you be able to do it?' I asked.

'I expect so,' he said. 'Anyway, we'll do our best.'

On the Saturday the crowd which we'd asked for assembled in large numbers. Although in those days on occasions, such as Guy Fawkes night, large numbers of undergraduates had to be controlled by the police, the relationship on both sides was friendly and accordingly quite a small number of policemen was capable of controlling a large crowd. So it happened on this occasion and the police were most helpful. For example, when we found that some of the crowd were too near the villain and the heroine, we asked the police if they would keep them back a little and they duly obliged. In the result, when the film was shot, there was a picture of the villain tying up the heroine and a policeman holding the crowd back. The film was duly shown and certainly we, as organisers, thought it was a great success. I was most grateful to the police and the senior proctor.

In the same year I was responsible with Norman Hartnell and others for writing the book of the Footlights Dramatic Club's May Week show called *The Bedder's Opera*. In it there was a song about the proctor of Cambridge. As Mr Hoskyns was obliging enough to get engaged to a Newnham girl shortly before the first performance, I added a special verse to this song for his benefit, and had the pleasure of seeing him and his fiancée listening to it from the dress circle of the no longer existing New Theatre, Cambridge.

The music for the show was written by M. D. Lyon, Brian

NOT OUT !

LYON MUST REMEMBER THAT NO PARTS OF THE BODY ARE ALLOWED TO PROTRUDE IN FRONT OF THE WICKET.

Davies and A. C. Ferguson. The first two were both law students.

M. D. Lyon was the well-known cricketer who kept wicket for Somerset in the twenties. He did not treat the law terribly seriously. I remember him telling me when he failed one of his Bar examinations that at the end of one paper he wrote: 'It's terribly hot in here, to take an examination at all, so if you've any doubt about passing me I think you should give me the benefit of it.' Unfortunately the examiners had no doubt about passing him and he was ploughed. Subsequently, however, he passed, was called to the Bar and eventually became a Colonial judge. He came back to England on retirement and died a few years ago. He was a very fine cricketer, a tuneful composer and a good companion. His other qualities were a very easy-going manner, great affability and a very prominent nose. Norman Hartnell drew a picture of him and his nose which I still have. It appears on page 16. I am grateful to Mr Hartnell for allowing me to have it reproduced.

Some time after the production of *Red Beaver* I had to obtain from my senior tutor, Dr Clapham (later Sir John Clapham), a certificate to enable me to receive payment of a leaving exhibition from my school. The certificate was in a somewhat archaic form. It required my tutor to say that I had 'behaved myself soberly, studiously and regularly'. On this occasion Dr Clapham, who did not approve of Kings men taking part in rags in the streets of Cambridge, said:

'Soberly? In the alcoholic sense of the word, perhaps. In other senses, disputed. Good morning.'

But he signed the certificate.

As against that, however, J. T. Sheppard, who subsequently became Provost, was talking about the definition of poetry to a gathering of undergraduates. He said that poetry could consist in any form of activity. It need not necessarily be in writing. 'For instance,' he said, 'making a film in the streets of Cambridge. That's poetry of a kind. A vulgar sort, if you like, but still poetry.'

*

It was, I think, much easier to pass the Bar examinations at the time when I was concerned with them than it is today. I did insufficient work for them and passed them all – in the third class. The first part of the examination I took when I was still at Cambridge and far more concerned with the activities of the Footlights Dramatic Club, with editing an undergraduate journal, with futile attempts to distinguish myself at rugger and tennis and with learning about people and things rather than about the law.

I once wrote in a book that, if a student worked reasonably hard for a Bar examination and still failed, it was unlikely that success at the Bar would be attained. Lord Parker, the then Lord Chief Justice, thereupon wrote to me that he had worked hard for the examination on Constitutional Law but had failed on the first occasion because he had read the wrong books. This strengthened me in my opinion that written examinations are a very unsatisfactory form of finding out whether a candidate has sufficient knowledge of the subject, because when he took the examination again, having read the right book, Lord Parker passed in the first class.

I live in Gray's Inn and my flat is only a few hundred yards from the premises of the Council of Legal Education. Mr Morrison, the Dean, had done me a number of favours and one morning a few years ago he asked me to do one for him. He told me that the lecturer, who normally welcomed the incoming students, had at the last moment been prevented from coming. He wondered whether I could come and take his place. I said I should be delighted to do so, provided the Dean did not mind what I said. He readily agreed to give me a free hand and I went round at the appointed time.

There was a large number of students and, having sympathized with them on the number of examinations they were going to take, I told them that I thought the present method of examination was all wrong. I said that the proper way to examine a student in any particular subject was for the examiner to invite him to come and have a cup of tea or a glass of sherry and over the tea or sherry, or, if he preferred it, tonic water, to discuss the subject of the examination. If in a friendly chat of about half an hour, say about contract, an examiner could not ascertain whether the student had done enough work and was of a high enough standard educationally to justify a pass in that subject, it would be the examiner who would be at fault and not the student. I ventured to say that, if there was a time when I knew any law, had I been the examiner, I should have been able to tell in that half-hour whether the student was entitled to pass the examination.

The Dean, in thanking me for my speech, said that he thoroughly approved of the idea. He said that the number of the intake that year was very large and that what he proposed to do with my consent was this. My flat was only a few minutes' walk from the Council's premises and he would arrange that at intervals of half an hour each student would call on me for the sherry, tea or tonic-water examination. He reckoned that, if I worked ten hours a day and six days a week, with a possible interval of, say, twenty minutes for my lunch in the middle – I would not need an interval for tea as that would be going on all the time – I might be able to get through the number of students taking the examination within about three months. He was most grateful for the suggestion.

This was a fair retort by the Dean, because the obvious objection to my method is that there are wholly insufficient examiners to enable the Council to put it into practice.

❖ Pupil

The second part of the Bar examinations I took shortly after I had come down from Cambridge and when I had already become a pupil of a junior barrister in the Temple.

Barristers are divided into Q.C.s (or K.C.s) and juniors. The junior is not necessarily young. He may become a High Court judge without ever taking silk (i.e. becoming a Q.C.).[1] The main difference between a junior and a Q.C. is that, whereas a junior does all the work of a barrister, i.e. advising about a case from beginning to end, preparing the necessary technical documents and finally arguing the case in court, a Q.C. for the most part only does the work in court. In many cases Q.C.s do not appear at all.

Becoming a pupil is embarking on an apprenticeship. But there are certain important differences between the position of a pupil today and his position when I was called to the Bar. Although it was then a practical necessity to become a pupil, it was not a legal requirement. As soon as a person was called to the Bar he was entitled to conduct a case in court. Indeed some foolish uncles, who were solicitors, sent their nephews briefs on the day after they were called. Since 1965, however, not only must the prospective practising barrister first read as a pupil for at least six months, but he is not allowed to open his mouth in court until that six months of pupillage has expired.

Another difference between the position of a pupil when I

1. So called by reason of the fact that a junior wears a stuff gown and a Q.C. a silk one.

was called to the Bar and that of one today is that my father had to pay 110 guineas for me to read as a pupil, whereas since about 1960 most barristers accept pupils without charging a fee. The difficulty today is to find a barrister who has sufficient room in his chambers to take another pupil. This is a very real problem and the prospective barrister would be well advised to make enquiries at a very early stage through any channels open to him about the prospects of becoming a pupil.

Until 1965 not only was a pupil allowed to accept briefs of his own but he was allowed to 'devil' for his master. This was excellent practice for the pupil but very nerve-racking and grossly unfair to the client whose case was likely to be mishandled.

The legal year starts in October and two or three months before then my father had sent me to see H. M. Giveen (at that time Common Law junior counsel to the Treasury) whom he knew slightly, with a view to his advising me about becoming a pupil.

Giveen was one of the comparatively few junior counsel to the Treasury who did not become a High Court judge. This was not due to any deficiencies on his part, but to the fact that he was not a man in good health. He told me that he would be prepared to take me as a pupil but strongly advised me not to come. He said that the work that he did was far too heavy and that I ought to go to someone who had much lighter work, some of it in the County Court. He gave me an introduction to Robert Fortune, who was a junior with a large and varied practice. His chambers were at 4 Essex Court, Temple.

Fortune was a very odd man. He had started his career as a bank clerk in Coutts' Bank but at the age of about thirty he was called to the Bar. This was in 1911. In 1924 he was earning about £5000 a year, which in those days was a large income. He was a married man with four daughters, one of whom was unfortunately killed in the 1939–45 war, and he had a farm in the country. But his only real interest, apart from his family, seemed to be his work. He was an extremely hard worker. He did not drink or smoke and was obviously extremely economical in his living habits. He would take a taxi if it was necessary, but otherwise he would always go by public transport. As far as I could make out, he had no interest in music, the theatre, the cinema or reading. When judges made literary allusions he could only smile and say: 'If your Lordship pleases.' He never made any himself, although he did use very frequently different catch-phrases, such as 'in meal or in malt'.[1] He had a rather high-pitched voice and had certain idiosyncracies in his ordinary conversation which I am afraid I gave to Mr Grimes, a character in *Brothers in Law*, a book which I wrote in 1955. One of them was to say, if he or anyone else was criticizing someone's conduct, often a judge's:

'But there it is, my dear fellow, they will do these things, they will do these things.'

And if there was an allegation of sexual misconduct in a case:

'But there it is, my dear fellow, the fellows will be fellows and the girls will be girls.'

Fortune was a very persistent advocate and many of his clients thought the world of him. He was particularly good at building cases. He obviously knew a lot about bricks and mortar and so forth. He would go into meticulous detail in preparing these cases. Every pupil believes his master is a good lawyer and that he is good at drafting the technical legal documents called 'pleadings'. I was no exception, but I learned later that I was quite wrong. He was not a good lawyer and his pleadings, although passable, were certainly not first rate. But it is impossible for the ordinary pupil to tell his master's standard of ability in these respects.

Fortune was known in the profession as 'Frothy Bob', which in *Brothers in Law* was translated into 'Foaming Billy'. He certainly talked a lot and, as you can see the spray when some actors are declaiming on the stage, so you could see Frothy Bob's when he was in full spate. The story that he once splashed the Master before whom he was arguing a case in chambers is no doubt apocryphal.

1. For the possible origin of this phrase, see Megarry's *Second Miscellany at Law* at pp. 247–8. It is a perfect bedside book for lawyers and laymen.

I had already become Fortune's pupil when on 19th November 1923 I was called to the Bar by the Treasurer of Gray's Inn, Judge Ivor Bowen, K.C. The Benchers who sponsored my call were Sir Harold Smith, Lord Birkenhead's brother, and Bernard Campion, the Metropolitan Magistrate. I had been introduced to them by Fortune and I met them once only. They had not known me or my parents before and I saw each of them for about a quarter of an hour.

Some people may wonder why they were prepared to recommend me for call to the Bar after such a short acquaintance. The reason was this. The Bar is a very close corporation and I hope, though with some misgivings, that it will remain so. When I was called to the Bar, there were well under 2000 practising barristers. Now there are over 3000, and the number is still increasing. The trust which exists between reputable members of the Bar is absolute and, as Fortune was well known to both my sponsors as a reputable member of the profession, each of them was satisfied that he would not have introduced me to them, unless he in turn was satisfied that I was fit to be called to the Bar.

*

Prospects for a newly-called barrister today are very different from what they were on 19th November 1923. There was not then enough work to go round. Today there is more work than the Bar can cope with. There are two reasons for this dramatic change, which is comparatively new and may be said to have started in about 1958 when the provisions of the Legal Aid and Advice Act 1949 started to take effect. The upsurge of the fortunes of the Bar is due partly to this provision of Legal Aid and partly to the increase in crime. When I came to the Bar, if a barrister volunteered to do what was called 'poor persons' work in civil cases or undertook dock briefs or had doled out to him easy briefs for the prosecution at Sessions or Assizes (known as 'soup'), he was either not paid at all or received a trifling amount. Under the Legal Aid scheme he is very handsomely paid. In consequence anyone going to the Common Law Bar today has an excellent chance of making a substantial income as soon as he has completed the compulsory period of six months' pupillage. His income after this period may amount to anything from £1500 to £3000 for the first year and substantially more thereafter. There were no such prospects for young men called in 1923. I am referring to the ordinary young men who came to the Bar after leaving the university at the age of anything from twenty-one to twenty-five. There have been examples of older men who, having made a successful career in the city, took the necessary examinations and were called to the Bar and within a short time acquired a substantial practice, partly owing to their ability and inside knowledge of commercial affairs and partly owing to the fact that the City solicitors, who knew them, almost immediately sent them briefs.

But there are not many of them and they form no part of the body of average young men to whom I am referring. Even as late as 1953 the prospects of success were poor. In a survey made by a *Times* special correspondent and published in *The Times* on 13th August 1953 it was stated that the writer had made a survey in seven or eight leading sets of chambers of all available juniors in these chambers. He found that the earnings of barristers of three years' standing averaged under £250 per annum, that those of from five to nineteen years' standing were under £800 and those of twenty years' standing or more were £2700. Although Legal Aid had been introduced in 1949, it was not for about ten years from its introduction that its beneficial effect upon the legal profession began to be felt. But from then on not only had the average young barrister an excellent prospect of making a substantial income as soon as the six months' qualifying period of pupillage had been served, but many more scholarships and grants were available to the law student than were available when I came to the Bar. I think that the only financial assistance which I had from any source other than that of my parents was a leaving exhibition from my school which was prolonged for my year of pupillage. This amounted to between £30 and £40.

But now a successful career at the Bar is open to almost anyone who is able to pass the necessary examinations and to find chambers, although it is more difficult for women. When I came to the Bar there were hardly any women there. Mrs Helena Normanton was, I think, the first. The profession had only been open to them since 1919. Today there are many more, but it is harder for them to find chambers than it is for young men. One reason is the continuing prejudice against them. It is rather like women becoming members of men's clubs. (A minor reason is the problem of lavatory accommodation, but, now that many chambers have girl clerks or typists, there is less foundation for objections on this ground.)

There was no problem about becoming a pupil in my day or, indeed, in finding a seat in chambers after pupillage. When I left Fortune's chambers there were several other sets where I could have gone. But I shall always be glad that I went to Le Quesne's, not just because it was a very happy and pleasant set of chambers and because the clerk was anxious to do all he could to promote my practice, but mainly because it was there that I met Frank Gahan and for the first time learned to understand the law. I do not apologize for repeating once or twice in this book how much his friendship and his help meant to me.

When I first went into Fortune's chambers there were four other pupils. Two were young men slightly older than me, who eventually left the Bar but have since done extremely well in legal departments of the Civil Service. The third was a very much older man whose intelligence was insufficient to enable him to acquire a practice at the Bar. The fourth was a nice young Indian who, I believe, has done very well since then in his own country.

Not long afterwards two further pupils arrived. They were to be outstandingly successful. One was Frank Soskice, who is one of my oldest friends and whom I introduced to Fortune. He subsequently became Solicitor-General, Attorney-General and Home Secretary and is now Lord Stow Hill. The other was Rodger Winn, who sadly died not long ago. He became a Lord Justice of Appeal.

When you first start as a pupil you read through the briefs which have been sent to your master, or as many as you can.

We had been warned that everything we read was confidential and must not be disclosed to anyone else. Such advice is very necessary because, although many cases are of no interest to the public, there are bound to be some which are and it is very tempting to the average person to show to his friends and acquaintances that he is aware of interesting facts which are only known to a very few other people. Even a Chancellor of the Exchequer, Mr Dalton, was unable to resist this temptation.

I remember that one of the cases which excited my interest was a divorce case in which a rich baronet with the unattractive name of Drughorn was accused of adultery, and Fortune was appearing for the petitioner. He was to be led by Sir Edward Marshall Hall. To my great disappointment, although defending the case almost up to the last moment, Drughorn eventually capitulated.

In those days there were far fewer divorces and I had been brought up, like many other people of my age, to look upon divorce with disfavour. Adultery was a topic which was never mentioned in my home. I remember my feelings – of both shock and fascination at the same time – when I first saw a woman who admitted adultery. I had a similar sensation when I saw my first criminal. There was a man who was actually kept in a prison cell and not allowed to walk about free as I was. I think it might be a good idea if everyone at an early age were compelled to visit a prison. I remember my sudden fear when I had walked in through the main door and it was shut behind me, and, although I knew that they would open it for me when I wanted to go out, there was a kind of finality about the way in which the gate was closed. If there is a criminal inside most of us, mine comes out into the open when I write fictional stories about crime. If ever I had been minded to commit crimes myself, I think that the closing of the gate behind me when I first went into a prison would have been sufficient to deter me.

*

Some of the briefs we read contained very long instructions and many documents. I wondered how I could ever succeed in a profession where it was necessary to master so much information. For the benefit of any young people who may feel the same, I can say at once that after a few years' experience of reading papers and starting to learn how to apply the law to the facts stated in those papers, the size of the brief eventually proved no deterrent to an understanding of the case.

As a pupil I followed Fortune round from court to court and I was enjoined by him to take careful notes of everything that happened. A knowledge of shorthand would have been a great advantage but most barristers eventually develop their own shorthand. I soon learned that appearing in court with Fortune could be a terrifying experience. To begin with, I learned it from the experience of others. Fortune was an extremely busy man and often had cases in more than one court at the same time. The result was that he would leave a case in the middle and, if he had not a leader or an official junior, one of the pupils would be deputed to act as his junior and hold the fort while he was away.

'Just tell the judge the tale, my dear fellow, just tell the judge the tale,' he would say as he disappeared.

I had been warned about this by my fellow pupils, who told me to look out when I saw Fortune moving towards the end of counsel's row and holding a whispered conversation with the clerk.

'Don't you worry, my dear fellow, you'll be quite all right, quite all right,' he would say to the wretched pupil, who was about to be left before a High Court judge with a case which he was quite incapable of conducting. The butterflies in the tummy which athletes and jockeys experience before a race are nothing to what a pupil used to experience when his master ran away and left him before a High Court judge, like the Ghost in *Hamlet* – 'unhouseled, disappointed, unaneled'. If he had known everything about the case which he was left to conduct, he would still have been wholly unable to conduct it. As it was, he often only had a very incomplete knowledge of it.

I remember that on one occasion Fortune was led by Sir John Simon, while Sir Douglas Hogg, the present Lord

Hailsham's father, was leading the other side with a junior. The case lasted two days. Sir Douglas Hogg and his junior were in court the whole time. Sir John Simon was there for half an hour out of the two days. Part of the half-hour was taken up in conducting a whispered conversation with his clerk, which ended with: 'Get me a taxi. One that will go quick.' He spent most of the time for which he was paid for being in court at the House of Commons.

For two hours out of those two days I was the only representative of our side. I think that Sir John's brief was only marked 250 guineas, which was not a very large sum for him, but I was later told by Fortune that the clients didn't mind his absence in the least and that they were perfectly satisfied to be able to say to their friends and acquaintances that they had briefed the great Sir John Simon. The case was about docks and harbours and, although I had read the brief, I hardly understood any of it. I forget who the judge was, but I do remember that, while at first he treated me as though I were in the case and asked me a question or two, as soon as he realized that it was pure waste of time to invite me to deal with any aspect of it, he disregarded me entirely. No doubt in order to see that justice was done, he asked the questions which he thought Sir John Simon would have asked had he been present. But he got no part of the 250 guineas.

I can still remember my absolute terror when I knew that I was going to be left in charge of a case in the High Court. I am not exaggerating when I say that the sense of fear which I then experienced was comparable to that which I felt when I first came under enemy shellfire in the war. And the relief which I felt when Fortune returned was very like the relief which I felt when my battalion came out of the line and beyond the reach of enemy fire.

Brothers in Law was made into a film in which Ian Carmichael and Richard Attenborough and some other distinguished artists appeared. In the book and the film a young man called Roger Thursby, who had just been called to the Bar, was sent straight into court and not unnaturally made a fool of himself.

In one instalment of a radio series based on the book he went into court and appeared for the wrong side. I had done this myself, and can assure readers that, having started to open a case for a plaintiff and pointed out what a bad fellow the defendant was, it was a little embarrassing to have to start again on behalf of the defendant and say what a good fellow he was after all.

The book was mainly written for the purpose of entertainment but some of it was also intended as propaganda. A fair number of lawyers thought the book and the film were funny, but a few important members of the legal profession were not amused. I asked one of them why he objected.

'If you write things like that,' he said, 'the public will think they really happen.'

I replied: 'When you stop them really happening, I will stop saying that they do happen.'

I should like to be able to claim the credit for the introduction of the six months' compulsory period of pupillage, but I am sure that I am not entitled to do so. It was not until a good many years after *Brothers in Law* was published that the change was made and it was then made because the matter was becoming a public scandal. The increase in crime and the granting of Legal Aid had by then had their effect. Briefs were pouring in and there were not enough barristers to do them. In consequence, the profession yielded to the temptation of allowing pupils, as soon as they were called, to appear in what no doubt were considered 'small' cases. Whether a case is small or not depends upon the view of the person who is using the word. The clerk in a set of chambers might say to the pupil: 'Oh, Mr Jones, just go down to such-and-such a magistrates' court and do this little case of careless driving. Good experience for you.' No doubt it would be. But the wretched driver, whose driving character was in jeopardy, could be forgiven for taking a very dim view of a profession which sent him a wholly inexperienced, incompetent and possibly a rather stupid advocate.

So compulsory pupillage for six months was introduced in 1965. That is all too short a time in which to learn how the wheels go round, and the period ought really to be a year. That is none too long. I realize that young people today require to earn an income at the earliest possible moment. On the other hand, justice is such an important commodity that the professions who are concerned with it ought to do the best they can to see that it is administered as fairly as possible. The advantage of a prosperous Bar is obvious from the point of view of those who practise at it. The disadvantage is that work comes too easily and practitioners may not take sufficient trouble to do their work to the best of their ability. A compulsory period of twelve months' pupillage should raise the standard, and unfortunately this is highly desirable.

I can give an example of what an inexperienced young man can do for his client, because, even after my year's pupillage was over, I did it myself. Any law student, who happens to be reading this, should be able to place the year in which I did it.

I was briefed to appear on behalf of a husband who was charged with cruelty by his wife. She was asking for a separation and maintenance order on that ground. The case was to be heard in a magistrates' court just outside London. There was in my chambers a fat blue book called *Stone's Justices' Manual* and in it I discovered, as I thought, that, if a husband and wife were still living together, the wife could not get a separation order against him on the grounds of cruelty. Although this seemed grossly unreasonable, it appeared to be the law. I do not remember the exact nature of the cruelty alleged against my client, but in the instructions given to me by my solicitor it was stated that he denied any cruelty. Although some barristers and solicitors have a touching (and often unjustified) faith in the honesty of their clients, even at that early stage in my career I was quite prepared to find that the wife was telling the truth and that my client was not. But when the same instructions stated that the couple were still living together, I found it difficult to think that the husband could have been lying about such a matter. It would be so easy to prove that the couple were not living together by evidence from neighbours, the postman, the milkman and others. It seemed to me, therefore, that unless there were very unusual circumstances in the case and the couple were not in fact living together, my client was bound to win.

My solicitor and the husband and I travelled down to the court by train. On the journey I cross-examined the husband not about his cruelty but about the vital question whether they were still living together. In the end I was quite satisfied that he was telling the truth. I may say at once that, although at that stage in my career my view that a person was or was not telling the truth was of very little value indeed, it did happen in this case to turn out to be correct. The parties were still living together. When I had finished my cross-examination I told my client, possibly a little pompously, that I believed him.

'Don't you have to?' he asked.

'Oh dear me no,' I said. 'But I do.'

'Very kind, I'm sure,' he said.

He was about twice my age and may well have resented the slight air of superiority (I hope it was slight) which I may have shown.

'You'll be glad to hear, Mr Blank,' I said, 'that, as you and your wife are still living together, you are bound to win the case.' He asked me why I could be so sure and I told him that it said so in the blue book which I had brought with me.

'But hasn't she got a lawyer?' he asked.

'No doubt,' I said, 'but her lawyer can't have looked it up.'

I seem to remember my solicitor saying to the husband how lucky it was that he had taken his advice and allowed him to brief counsel. It was a very pleasant journey after that, and we were almost sorry for the poor wife. This was in the days when there was no Legal Aid and here she was paying out her good money to be represented by a lawyer in a case which had no prospects whatever of succeeding, even though she could prove that her husband *had* hurled two plates and a teacup at her, and knocked her down regularly twice a day. We came to the end of our journey and reached the court and I went in and sat in the seats reserved for advocates. I was glad to see that the clerk had in front of him a copy of *Stone's Justices' Manual*, but

I noticed that there was a slight difference between my copy and his. His was dated a year later. Just to be on the safe side I asked if I could borrow it and he lent it to me. I was horrified to find that in between the two editions the law had been changed and the gross injustice to wives had been remedied. A wife *could* now get a separation order against her husband on the ground of cruelty, even though they were still living together. I didn't have time to tell my client about this, as the case was called on a moment later, but at any rate I didn't make a fool of myself by taking a false point in court. I had to fight the claim on the merits and I duly lost it. Whether the husband or I could claim the chief credit for this I cannot say after so many years, but if a tape-recording of the case were available I should be surprised if I could listen to it without discomfort. When the case was over we left the court and I explained to my client how it was that I had not taken the point about which I had been so optimistic in the train. I thought he behaved rather decently. All he said when we parted was: 'Well, goodbye and thank you. But next time, son, get the latest edition.'

I think that the most important piece of advice which Fortune gave me was this. 'Make certain,' he said, 'that you bring out the whole of your case in evidence.'

This may seem pretty obvious advice to give, but, unless you have been given it and appreciate the desirability of acting on it, it is very easy to leave out something of importance. Where your witness is difficult to handle and where the judge is impatient, in your early days you are so anxious to sit down and to be rid of the task of examining the witness that you may easily fail to ask him a vital question. Particularly when it looks as though you are going to lose a case, it is essential to follow the advice which I have mentioned, but it is often very difficult to do so. You are appearing, say, for the defendant, the judge appears to have accepted the evidence of the plaintiff's witnesses and one or more of your witnesses has been cross-examined into the ground. In such circumstances, in my early days I often wished that the case was over. The agony involved in slowly losing is great. As nail after nail is hammered into your coffin you devoutly wish that the last nail had been driven home and the coffin lowered into the ground. Even where the judge is not impatient, it is difficult enough to keep going full steam ahead, but, where it becomes obvious that the judge appears to have made up his mind against you, there are few inexperienced advocates who are not tempted to run away and not very many who resist the temptation. Mr Justice Swift had a nasty habit of tapping his desk with a pencil when he wanted you to stop. Sometimes the tapping would be punctuated by such helpful questions as 'Is that your best point?' or 'You've said that before'. Swift, in fact, did not often use the last phrase because at that stage he was probably not listening and so he was unaware of the fact that you were repeating yourself.

But worse than losing a case which never looked much like a winner is when dark clouds suddenly appear in a previously clear sky followed by a burst of 'black rain and fire and hail'. Particularly when the invocation to the judge to hear is no more effective than Shelley's cry to the west wind. This sort of thing is inclined to happen when proofs have been carelessly taken by a solicitor or his clerk. A proof is a statement of a witness which is given to counsel by his instructing solicitor. It has originally been obtained by the solicitor or one of his clerks and it normally starts with, 'JOHN JONES WILL STATE:'. According to the ability and experience of the prooftaker, 'will state' may represent the truth or it may be a piece of optimism or merely a pious hope. Occasionally 'will not state' would be more accurate.

Although a lawyer who says that he wins all his cases is either guilty of gross exaggeration or has a very small practice indeed, anyone who is able and experienced ought to win substantially more civil cases than he loses, for one very good reason. If he is any good at prophesying the result of a case, he will persuade his clients to settle a very doubtful case at an early stage. And if, after some years of experience, he is not a good judge of the prospects of success in civil cases he ought to leave the Bar and go in for something else.

B

⊞ 4 Essex Court, Temple

Although my powers of physical description are very limited, I think that in *Brothers in Law* I gave a fairly accurate picture of what the chambers at 4 Essex Court looked like when I said in effect that the method of cleaning was for a lady called a 'laundress' to come round early every morning, make herself a cup of tea and then go on to the next set of chambers. Although there was some improvement in the appearance of chambers in the Temple between 1923 and 1939, it took Hitler's bombs to make a real change for the better.

There were three permanent members of the chambers besides Fortune. The head of the chambers was R. F. Colam, K.C., who was Recorder of Croydon. He was an example of a barrister who had quite a good junior practice but who failed as a silk. A man may be very successful as a junior because he is first class at advising and drafting and reasonably efficient as an advocate without being outstanding. But, if he is to succeed as a Q.C., his standard of advocacy must be high. If it is very high he will go to the top. But if it is only moderate he may fail altogether.

Although Colam was quite a forceful advocate, so is a bull, and the comparison is not entirely unfair, either as regards Colam's physique or behaviour in court. He was a shortish, well-built man with a heavyish face and he was inclined to lower his head and charge. He did not have very much work when I came into the chambers and by the time he retired a few years later he had practically none. The other two members were Henry Dickens, a grandson of the novelist, who became a personal friend of mine and an Irishman called Sir Alfred Callaghan.

Some of the criticisms which I make about barristers and judges whom I got to know in my early days will be made as a result of hindsight, but even at the age of twenty-one and with no experience at the Bar I had no difficulty in seeing that Sir Alfred Callaghan was remarkably unintelligent for a lawyer. He had a large red hooked nose, but its colour was due to dyspepsia rather than alcohol, which he did not touch. The rest of his head wasn't much larger than his nose. So there wasn't very much room in it. He was a considerable talker and took a very long time to say nothing at all. When he had no work, he would come into the pupils' room and waste our time by telling us over and over again what a beautiful and rich woman his wife was. He seemed to be immensely proud of living in an hotel, for he was forever referring to the fact that he and his wife lived at the Hotel Victoria in Northumberland Avenue (now, like Sir Alfred, defunct).

Most people who were unaware of his antecedents thought he must be an Irish baronet, because they couldn't conceive how he could have achieved the distinction of knighthood. He had apparently obtained it for secret services to the Liberal party, for whom he was at one time a candidate. His knighthood certainly stood him in good stead at the Bar, for it is difficult to think that he would have got anywhere at all but for the fact that solicitors' managing clerks felt upgraded by having conferences with 'Sir Alfred', while a few County Court judges, although they could not always understand his oft-repeated and often unintelligible arguments, were quite pleased to have counsel in their courts whom they could address as 'Sir Alfred'. It seemed to raise the standard of the court.

Sir Alfred would never, if he could avoid it, appear by himself in the High Court. He was far too nervous. On the rare occasions when he was absolutely compelled to appear without a leader his hands shook so much that he could hardly turn over the pages of his brief. He was not a young man, though at the age of twenty-one I would have said this about anybody over thirty-five. I think he was probably between fifty and sixty, and it was embarrassing even for an inexperienced and ignorant person like myself to hear him trying to present a case intelligibly without having the slightest chance of being able to do so. High Court judges treated him in a kindly manner, not because he was Sir Alfred but because from their point of view, even though they may have been his age or older, he was a poor, miserable frightened man who was at their mercy. He was a very different character in the County Court, because there he spoke his nonsense with confidence. I don't think I actually devilled for Sir Alfred while I was still a pupil, but when I stayed on in chambers after my pupillage was over, he would sometimes say: 'Just do this little possession case for me, would you? I've got a big case in another court. It'll be good practice for you, my boy.' It certainly was excellent practice for me, but this could have been no consolation to the person whose case I lost. It is also true that, however bad the representation, the judge will do his best to arrive at a fair decision and probably in 70 per cent to 80 per cent of cases will succeed in doing so. But 20 per cent is a very large number and in the days when I appeared in County Courts I lost cases which I ought to have won when I was against a superior opponent. Later on, when I was more experienced, I probably won cases which I ought not to have won.

Henry Dickens was far and away the most worthwhile person in the chambers. He could have acquired a very substantial practice but he had interests outside the Bar and was also too idle by nature. He did, however, a lot of work for the Medical Defence Union. He was a forthright, courageous and able advocate, who in spite of his admirable combative qualities, remained always on the best of terms with his opponents. Many doctors must have been thankful for his skill and determination in court and his sound, robust advice outside. He was immensely kind and helpful to younger men. I shall always remember with gratitude his advice and encouragement and, most prized of all, his friendship.

The clerk was the oldest, or second oldest, clerk in the Temple and his name was Williams. He was a very nice old man and, when the time came for him to bring me my first brief, he offered it to me like a faithful old family retainer bringing a drink to his master on a beautiful silver salver and in spite of his shaking hand not spilling a drop. (I once spent about an hour in the chair of a dentist who suffered from palsy or something of that sort, and whose hands shook like Sir Alfred Callaghan's when in the High Court. It was a frightening experience when the dentist started to use the drill. Nevertheless, though his hand was shaking considerably the whole time, he never once made a mistake and the job was done as perfectly and as painlessly as if it had been done by somebody with a steady hand. Since then I have ceased to be surprised by palsied waiters who serve you with soup without noticeably spilling it down your back.)

It was in 1924 that Williams brought me my first brief. It was from a solicitor whom my parents knew and I was instructed to give an opinion about a Will. It was a very pleasant feeling to see my name on the outside of a brief. I think the fee was two guineas. I read the instructions and I must say that they read very much like an examination paper. I had not much difficulty in looking up the answer in a law book and I still do not know whether the solicitor had invented the whole thing in order to be nice to me.

Frank Soskice started his career at the Bar a little after mine. We had been at Colet Court and St Paul's School together. He had always been a Socialist and I had always been a Conservative. When I was a pupil of Fortune, I had no thoughts of becoming a judge. I had mild political aspirations, that is to say, I should have liked to have become Prime Minister. With this in mind I joined the United Club and sometimes spoke for Conservative candidates at elections.

My father was a mathematician and he was a good and kind man, rather self-effacing and well read in the English classics. Although he was not an expert on political economy, nor indeed on any aspect of politics, he was a very strong Conservative. My mother was a much more forceful character and equally well read but did not really consider that women should have political views except those of their husbands. My parents being good Conservatives, I was one too. Anything my father said on the subject I would repeat with confidence as being my view. Frank questioned my views and it was very good for me. From him I learned a lot, and one thing in particular – to ask the question 'Why?'. It is funny how isolated events of no particular importance can remain in one's memory. My family lived in Bayswater and I remember that, when we were fourteen or fifteen, Frank and I were walking along the road which runs between Porchester Terrace and Queensway (which was then called Queen's Road) and during our conversation I said that it would be absurd to have crossing-sweepers who could read Homer.

'Why?' asked Frank.

Although it may sound a simple thing to learn to ask why, it is of the greatest value both in the legal profession and in life generally. 'Why?' and 'Why not?' are two questions which every experienced advocate asks of his clients.

'Did you think that Mrs Jones was sexually attractive?'

'Yes.'

'Did you ever kiss her?'

'Yes.'

'Did you ever commit adultery with her?'

'No.'

'Did you ever ask her to commit adultery with you?'

'No.'

'Why not?'

If no satisfactory answer could be given to that question the probability is that at least one of the previous answers was a lie.

Frank and I had no money when we started at the Bar, but we each had a home, so that we never had to go hungry. On the other hand it is much nicer for a young man to have food out sometimes and in those days it was far less expensive than it is today. I remember that on one occasion we only had about 10d each but we were able to find a restaurant where we could dine for this amount. There was a restaurant in Soho called Molinari's where you could have a five-course dinner for 1s 6d (7½p). The food was pretty bad and we only went there once or twice, preferring to pay 1s 6d, if we had as much, for a better three-course dinner elsewhere. Often we went to Chinese restaurants where you could fill yourself for a very small sum.

One way in which I supplemented my meagre income in my first years at the Bar was by writing articles on motoring law. At that time there was a car called the Clyno, and the company which manufactured it produced a magazine called *The Great Highway*. A friend of mine who was concerned with the company asked whether I was prepared to write articles for it for four guineas an article. I readily agreed and, after having written an article or two for *The Great Highway*, I thought I might try my luck with some of the other motoring magazines. I sent in one or two articles to *The Autocar*, *The Motor* and *The Light Car & Cycle Car* and I heard nothing from them, only to discover a month or two later that all the articles had been published. I sent in an account to each of the magazines charging £3 per article. They all said that that was above their normal rate (which was about half that amount) and that, if I wanted a special rate, I must say so when I sent the article. So I said so and became a regular contributor to all these magazines. In consequence, I could always make £3 by writing on some aspect of motoring law. I should think that altogether I must have written about a hundred such articles. The resultant income was a great help to me. Although some young barristers may do the same sort of thing today, I doubt whether it is necessary or whether they have the time.

At the end of my pupillage I stayed on in Fortune's chambers and Frank went to the chambers of H. D. Samuels, a junior with a large practice in insurance work. He did well from the start, although his refusal to accept anything which was not firmly established as right made him appear a somewhat unusual practitioner. After he had been practising for a year or two I remember meeting Fox-Andrews, one of the busy juniors for whom I used to devil, and he said:

'I saw an extraordinary chap the other day. He asked a lot of incredible questions.'

I said: 'Was his name Soskice?'

'By jove, it was,' he said. 'I've never seen anything like it. He'll never get on like that.'

I had no doubt of his eventual success and said so. Fox-Andrews expressed great surprise, not to say disbelief.

'You will see,' I said. And in due course he did.

⊞ Circuit Judges

Circuit judges did not exist in name until after the passing of the Courts Act 1971, but it is a convenient title for a chapter which deals with County Court judges, permanent judges at the Old Bailey and Chairmen of Quarter Sessions, all of whom are now known as Circuit judges, though not when I was a judge.

The first time I heard my voice in court was in a County Court before an irascible judge called Crawford. He was a disappointed man who thought he was fit to be a High Court judge and was continually trying to impress his erudition upon people in the court. He liked to have as big an audience as possible. In consequence, although it might be obvious that he could not possibly get through his list during the day, he would refuse applications for adjournments until the end of the day, when half the cases in his list would have to be adjourned.

I once had a case before him about a tailor's bill for which the sum claimed was something like ten or twelve pounds. I had to attend twice at Romford County Court and twice at Ilford County Court before the case was finally heard. This sort of thing is unheard of today. Indeed, the English County Court is probably one of the most efficient courts in the world, in that cases are heard very shortly, i.e. six to seven weeks, after the summons has been issued, and they are always heard on the day which is fixed for the trial, unless, of course, there is some good reason for the cases being adjourned.

My opponent in my first case was S. R. Sidebottom, who

subsequently, when he got tired of anonymous telephone calls
asking him what he was going to do about it, changed his name
to Edgedale. He later became a County Court judge, and sometimes sat in the second court at Willesden County Court,
where I had become the senior judge in 1953. He was a much
quicker judge than I was and a very much better judge of
character. He died all too soon and it needed at least one and a
half judges to replace him.

There is a very odd feeling when you first open your mouth
in court. I could hear my voice resounding in the rafters. I knew
that it was I who was speaking but it all felt rather unreal.

Fortunately for me on this occasion the case involved a short
point of law on which the judge thought (probably rightly)
that the argument which I was instructed to put forward was
correct. Flushed with success, I proceeded to ask the judge for
an order which he had no power to make.

In one's early days at the Bar the winning or losing of a case
is of vital importance to one's own self-esteem. On the way
home from losing a case I would, like, I suspect, many other
young people, convince myself that I couldn't have won and,
when I thought of some point which I had failed to take and
which might have completely changed the fortunes of my
client, I found excellent reasons for my not having taken it.
This process would go on all the way in the train from the
County Court to the Temple.

When I went into court in my early days, I very much
appreciated any kindly word from anybody connected with the
court. More than once in going to a magistrates' court I have
been encouraged by a friendly remark about the weather from
a man whom I took to be the clerk of the court. The clerk of the
court in a magistrates' court is a very important person, even
when there is a stipendiary magistrate sitting. But when there
is a Bench of J.P.s he is the authority on law in the court and,
although they are not bound to take his advice on legal matters,
they usually do. On two of these occasions the man whom I
thought to be the clerk turned out to be the usher. However, it
served its purpose and I felt better for being able to agree that

it was a lovely day or, alternatively, that it had been a terrible summer.

After some years of practice and devilling for other people in County Courts, instead of hoping that I wouldn't have to do the case myself, I hoped that I would. I would prepare a case carefully and go down to a County Court to hold the fort for someone else. Believing, no doubt wrongly, that I was fully capable of conducting the case in an efficient manner, I would pray that the man whose case it was would not turn up. Sometimes he never did, and that was fine – unless I lost the case. But when he suddenly turned up just before the case was called it was a very great disappointment. All I could do was to watch how he conducted it and to try and learn something in that way.

I remember on one occasion that I was asked by a well-known junior called B. L. O'Malley to devil a case for him at Bow County Court. It was a squabble between two neighbours and I know that it had something to do with a parrot. O'Malley had said to me that the one thing I must do was to keep the plaintiff in the witness-box until he arrived to cross-examine him on behalf of the defendant. Fortunately for me a deputy judge was sitting and in spite of the fulminations of my opponent at what he described – quite rightly – as my wasting the time of the court, I was able to keep the witness in the witness-box in time for O'Malley to come along and demolish him.

O'Malley always remembered this occasion and very kindly gave me full credit for it. He had a large practice and I did quite a lot of devilling for him. He lived to a great age and continued to practise almost up to his death. Unfortunately he went on too long. He had been an able advocate and a very successful practitioner, but his years were too many for him and I found it very embarrassing when sometimes he appeared before me when I was a County Court judge. I really don't know why solicitors continued to brief him, because they must have realized that often he could not get the hang of the case at all. I also had the lesser embarrassment of Fortune appearing before me when I was sitting as a Divorce Commissioner. But,

as the cases in which he appeared before me were only undefended divorce cases, nothing much could go wrong.

*

Good representation in a County Court is of vital importance.
Naturally some County Court judges are better than others,
but very few of them attain the standard of a High Court judge.
In the High Court, representation is less important, because the
standard of judge is higher and most cases will be decided in the
same way, however disparate the ability of counsel on one side
may be from that of counsel on the other.

Judge Snagge, the father of the rowing blue and B.B.C.
commentator, was probably the best County Court judge
before whom I appeared. Many practitioners thought that he
ought to have been a High Court judge. As far as I could tell,
he had all the qualities of a first-class judge. He was a good
lawyer, quiet, courteous, but nevertheless quick. He said very
little, possibly even too little. By this I mean that, if a judge says
nothing at all, neither side can tell how his mind is working and
it is very important for an advocate to know this. It is not all
that easy for a judge in the County Court to keep quiet. Sometimes only one side is represented by a lawyer and then he is
bound in most cases to ask questions which the unrepresented
litigant should have asked. Similarly, when the standard of
representation is low, the judge is forced to take a more vocal
part in the case. Judge Snagge was exceptional, because somehow or other he managed to try his cases extremely well
without taking more than a very minor speaking part.

Few people today will remember the County Court judges
before whom I used to appear in my early days. I suppose that
one of the best known was Sir Alfred Tobin at Westminster
County Court. He had unsuccessfully defended Crippen, the
murderer. It was from Tobin that I learned to like oysters. I
had a case before him in which my opponent was a young man
called Graham Swanwick (now a High Court judge). It was not
a simple case and would take some time to try. Tobin had not
started it by half past twelve and at that moment he sent a

note down to me and my opponent asking us if we would lunch with him at the adjournment. We were naturally very pleased to do so and at one o'clock he took us to Scott's and there he gave us two dozen oysters and two pints of draught stout, and I must say that they went down very well together. Shortly before three we left the restaurant to go back to the court. On the way Tobin said to us: 'Of course you boys will settle your case.' But to our credit be it said that, though we tried, we were not able to do so. Tobin, who hadn't the slightest intention of trying a difficult case at that hour of the day after a good lunch, knew how to deal with this situation.

'Would you mind,' he said, 'if I saw your lay clients privately by myself?'

I don't know what Swanwick said to his client but I said to mine that I was very sorry about it, that the judge had no intention of trying the case that day, and that, if he refused to go and see him, the case would simply be adjourned to another day, which would involve additional costs, but that, if he did go in and see him, Tobin would force him and his opponent to agree to some compromise, whether they liked it or not. My client said that he would go and see the judge. Swanwick's client also agreed and ten or fifteen minutes after they had gone in, they came out with the case well and truly settled. I have no recollection what the case was about or whether the settlement was a fair one. But what I really remember is that I have liked oysters ever since.

Another judge was Spencer Hogg (no relation of Lord Hailsham) whose main defect was that he did not like sitting after lunch. One day I had a difficult fraud case in front of him. He spent the morning dealing with small applications and persuading various people to settle their cases and eventually at one o'clock he adjourned for lunch. We came back at two and I started to open the case. I had not gone very far when he said:

'You know, I've had a very heavy morning and I've got a bit of a cold, so I think I'll adjourn now.' And the case was duly adjourned at the expense of the parties.

I have already mentioned Crawford, whose complete dis-

regard of other people's convenience made him deservedly
unpopular, but his unpopularity was nothing to that of a judge
called Hill Kelly, who began to sit at Bloomsbury County
Court when he left Cardiff to the great relief of practitioners
there. Hill Kelly was a man with a considerable knowledge of
County Court practice, a fair knowledge of the law and a pretty
strong belief in his own infallibility. The great reason for his
unpopularity among lawyers was because he required the law
and practice to be observed to the nth degree. Unfortunately in
the County Court it is by no means universal for practitioners
to come into court with full knowledge of the rules of court
which are going to apply to the cases with which they are
concerned. They did not have long to wait before Hill Kelly
would say, for example: 'What about Order IX, Rule 8?'
Personally I found his attitude towards us a great advantage
because it compelled me to learn the practice. It also compelled
me to apply my mind to the rules of evidence in cases where
proof of certain facts would readily be accepted in most courts
but not without argument before Judge Hill Kelly. The cases
before Hill Kelly always required the most meticulous prepara-
tion. But he was extremely rude in the way in which he
showed off his own knowledge and showed up the ignorance of
others. Whether or not he enjoyed hurting other people's
feelings I don't know. He certainly did not mind doing so. The
time came when solicitors refused to appear in front of him and
when his own Registrar, Mr Registrar Friend, asked for a
transfer. Mr Registrar Friend was a second-rate humorist. He
was always making remarks which found their way into the
evening papers. No doubt Hill Kelly allowed appeals from
some of his decisions and was probably extremely unpleasant to
him privately. Eventually Friend obtained a transfer to
Clerkenwell County Court.

But my objection to Hill Kelly was that he was not in the
least interested in the attainment of justice, only in applying
legal rules and regulations. This was bad enough when both
parties were represented before him, but, when litigants appeared
before him personally and were treated in the same way as

advocates, the result was disgraceful. I have seen the tenant of a house, who brought a claim for possession against her sub-tenant on some ground or other, go into the witness-box. This was long before the days of Legal Aid and she probably had insufficient money with which to instruct a solicitor. So she had to do the case herself. She had obviously never been in court before and was extremely nervous. Once she had taken the oath she waited for something to happen. So did the judge. Eventually he said:

'Well, ma'am?'

The woman did not know what to say, so she still said nothing.

'Struck out,' said Hill Kelly. 'Call the next case.'

More than once complaints were made by solicitors to the Lord Chancellor about Hill Kelly's conduct. Nothing resulted from these complaints. But presumably nobody mentioned to the Lord Chancellor the way in which the wretched litigants were treated if they were not represented in his court. If this had been mentioned, it would have been interesting to know whether the Lord Chancellor would have had power to remove him. A County Court judge could then and can now only be removed on the ground of 'inability or misbehaviour'. I should have thought that, if a sufficient number of cases like the one I have mentioned had been presented to the Lord Chancellor and properly vouched for, he might have been entitled to say that this amounted to misbehaviour.

One piece of good advice, which I heard Hill Kelly give, has lasted me since he gave it. No doubt some readers heard it when they first went to school. I had a case in which I thought that there might be difficulty in giving strict proof of some fact which was essential to my client's success. It was a purely technical point which most judges would not have worried about. But I knew that, if I failed to prove it before Hill Kelly, he would entirely disregard the merits of my client's case and dismiss it for want of proof. I was appearing for the plaintiff and I advised my client that the only way of being certain to be able to prove the matter in question was to issue a witness summons on the defendant himself. As I have said, it was a purely technical matter and the defendant in the witness-box would have been bound to give the necessary evidence in our favour. I told my solicitors to issue a witness summons and to serve it upon the defendant before he arrived at the court. This they did. In due course I called all my evidence to prove everything that was required of me with the exception of this one technical matter. I could see (or thought I could see) a gleam in Hill Kelly's eye which showed that he was all ready to take the point against me. So I called the defendant to give evidence on the plaintiff's behalf. Apart from formal questions I asked him only one question to which he gave the answer which I required. I then sat down.

The course which I had taken was one to be avoided unless it was essential, because it gave the opportunity to the advocate on the other side to cross-examine his own witness. But the solicitor in the present case did not appreciate his advantage. When I sat down, he rose and, looking very uncomfortable, said:

'This puts me in a difficulty, your Honour.'

'Difficulties,' said Hill Kelly, 'were made to be overcome.'

I rather feel that Christ might have said this before changing the water into wine.

Hill Kelly had no better manners outside court than he had inside. I was walking with my wife in Kensington Gardens once when we met him. I duly raised my hat and he raised his umbrella in return.

*

I occasionally went to the Old Bailey where there were then three permanent judges, the Recorder, Sir Ernest Wild, the Common Serjeant, Sir Henry Dickens (a son of Charles Dickens and father of the Dickens in Fortune's chambers) and Judge Atherley Jones. Today there are between twenty and thirty judges.

I remember very well my first case before Sir Ernest Wild. He could be as smooth as glass or as biting as a cuttlefish. My first case before him was for a man called Hector Lyon, who was otherwise known as Hector Rayner Sutherland Leveson-Gower. He was charged (not for the first time) with fraud. It was what is called a long-firm fraud. This consists of buying goods on credit and then selling them cheaply for cash and not paying the people from whom they were bought. Wild was extremely nice to young men unless they crossed him in some way and I managed to avoid his displeasure on that occasion. (In the result I thought that my career had really started when he very kindly sent my mother the posy which at that time judges at the Old Bailey carried into court.)

The allegation against my client was that he had obtained large quantities of toffee by false pretences. (He must indeed have had a sweet tooth, for, when he was on remand in custody, he begged his solicitor not to forget to send him some jam.) Before credit was given by one of the suppliers to the accused he was asked for references and one of the references which he gave was from a man who was stated to be the Baron de Pitchford. In his reference the Baron said what an excellent customer Hector Lyon would be and added that 'knowing him as I do I cannot well say less'. The only knowledge which the Baron de Pitchford in fact had of Hector Lyon was that they were both serving sentences of penal servitude in Dartmoor prison when they met. When my client was being cross-examined in the witness-box by counsel for the prosecution he was most unfairly asked: 'Where did you meet the Baron de Pitchford?' To which he replied: 'In Devonshire, sir.'

After I had been at the Bar a little over a year I used to wear a top hat and I think that my wearing it dates from this case of Hector Lyon. I was just twenty-two. When I went to the Old Bailey I wanted to meet my solicitor client and I asked one of the janitors if he had seen Mr Thomas.

'No,' he replied. 'Why? Are you his clerk?'

It seemed to me that a top hat was the answer to that.

Another young practitioner who used to wear a top hat was the present Lord Pearce. I always remember him dashing around with his top hat and his blue bag.

A blue bag is the bag in which a barrister carries his robes

when he starts his career. Later on, when he is led by a Q.C.,
he is likely to be given a red one, if his leader thinks that his
conduct of the case merits it. I once wrote in a book about the
law (*Brief to Counsel*) that, although plenty of barristers who
were presented with red bags were never made judges, no one
with a blue bag was ever made one. A High Court judge
thereupon wrote to me and said that he had never received a
red bag. I in fact received my red bag from Roland Oliver,
K.C., who subsequently became Mr Justice Oliver.

There was a curious old judge – they all appeared old to me
– called Judge Bairstow. He had a strong North Country
accent and was very rough and ready in his methods. He
obviously disliked the trappings of the law.

'Don't say "with respect" to me,' he would frequently tell
counsel. 'You don't mean it.'

When first I appeared in front of him I treated him like any
other judge and lost nearly all my cases. But I soon realized
that he liked counsel to address him in a more colloquial
manner and to leave out the 'with respects' and the 'your
Honours' and the subservience which one usually adopted
towards the Bench. So I used to talk to him in a completely
conversational manner, which he obviously preferred. But I still
lost most of my cases in front of him.

One of the nicest and least efficient of the judges was Judge
Sturges. He was a great horseman and I'm sorry that I never
had a case in front of him which involved horses. He would
certainly have decided in favour of the horse. But he taught me
one thing, and that was never to go into court without taking
with me all the authorities on which I wanted to rely and never
to rely simply on a statement in a textbook about an authority.
In my early days of practice I had a case in front of him in
which my client had no merits but in which he was technically
in the right. Judge Sturges, like most judges, preferred to find
in favour of the person with the merits. I quoted a case from a
textbook which showed that the law was in my favour, but
Sturges ignored the case and found against me. Subsequently I
applied to him for a new trial and on this occasion I produced

the authority in question. My opponent admitted and the judge was constrained to admit also that in fact his decision was wrong in law. But he refused to grant me a new trial on the ground that he had no power to do so and that the only method of testing this decision in law was by appealing to the High Court. As I needed leave to appeal to the High Court in the particular case and he had refused to give it to me, my client was left without a remedy. And although my client suffered no moral injustice he certainly suffered a legal injustice.

I never went into court again anywhere without taking with me every authority on which I might conceivably want to rely. This sometimes involved taking a very large number of books to the County Court, because you could never be quite sure whether one or other of them might be required. In order not to frighten the judge with them I often used to leave the bulk of them and sometimes all of them in the robing room and only send for any of them if it became necessary. On one occasion the carriage of these books may have saved my life. I was driving to Brighton County Court with a vast number of them in the dickey of the car and a rear tyre burst and the weight of the books kept the car from overturning.

The case in question was a claim by a landlord against a tenant and was heard by Judge Moore Cann. My opponent was J. D. Casswell. The case involved consideration of some highly technical legal points relating to the law of landlord and tenant. Both Casswell and I prepared our arguments most carefully and each of us made very long submissions in which we cited most of the cases which we'd brought. In consequence of our researches and our tenacity the case took four days. At the end of it the judge reserved judgment and eventually we went down to hear it. It was very short. The judge recited the facts and then said:

'The Plaintiff said that an oil painting ran as the result of water coming through the roof. Now,' said the judge, 'oil paintings cannot run. I therefore reject the evidence of the plaintiff and decide in favour of the defendant.' That was in effect the whole of his judgment. My opponent and I might have left all the cases at home and said nothing about them at all. However, personally, I learned a lot and it may be that my life was saved.

Another judge, Judge Turner, was a comic sort of judge. He tried his cases very quickly, which was not altogether surprising, as he had been a great athlete and had got a blue for running a mile. His form of justice was very rough and ready and anything could happen in his court.

On one occasion a young member of the Bar quoted a case in favour of his client and submitted that the case showed that his client was in the right. Whereupon, to the young man's consternation, his opponent pointed out to the judge that that case had been overruled in the Court of Appeal. Turner leaned forward towards the young counsel:

'That's a bit of a b——, isn't it?' he said sympathetically.

In those days there was a procedure by which a judgment creditor could try and make his debtor pay by obtaining an order of imprisonment against him suspended so long as he paid so much a week or so much a month. The method by which the creditor attempted to do this was by the issue of a judgment summons. Thousands of these judgment summonses were issued and they all had to come before the judge. Normally they took a long time. The court would be crowded with debtors and usually a whole morning at least would be occupied by hearing these cases. Turner had a simple way of dealing with them.

'Hands up those debtors who are prepared to pay so much a month,' he would say. The amount would not be very large and a good number of hands would go up.

'Who's for the creditors?' he would ask, and one or two solicitors rose.

'D'you accept?' Turner would say. 'If so, an order will be made in your cases. If not they will go to the bottom of the list and I will hear them later.'

Solicitors soon realized that, even if they did wait until the case was eventually reached, Turner would probably make the same order. So they usually agreed in the first instance.

Judgment summonses have been a source of oppression to many judges, but they were no problem to Judge Turner.

Judge Cluer, who presided at Shoreditch and Whitechapel County Courts, did not like his Jewish customers. He would almost invariably prefer the evidence of a witness who was not a Jew. I remember once appearing in a case before him and confidently calling my next witness.

'Call Mr Brown,' I said. The witness went into the box. Cluer glanced at him.

'B-r-a-u-n,' said Cluer, and he was right.

*

In 1973, with a view to making County Court procedure less formal, less expensive and less terrifying to people outside the legal profession and much simpler and quicker, the Lord Chancellor introduced what may be not unfairly termed a revolutionary set of rules. These rules enable the judge in any case and the registrar in cases where the claim does not exceed £75, to order that the case should be tried by way of arbitration either before the judge or registrar or before some outside person, whether a lawyer or not, if either party applies for such an order. In such arbitrations strict rules of evidence need not be observed and the parties will be discouraged from having legal assistance by the rule that, whether they win or lose, there will be virtually no legal costs of the hearing. As far as I understand it, the only requirement of the arbitration is that the methods of natural justice shall be observed. For example, if a judge were foolish enough to say that he always preferred the evidence of a man to that of a woman or that he always preferred the evidence of a driver to that of a pedestrian, there would be some method no doubt of upsetting the decision. But, provided the judge only thinks these things and never gives expression to them, his decision will be unassailable. It remains to be seen how satisfactorily this scheme will work.

Undoubtedly the costs of litigation are far too high and the average person cannot afford them. But this is inevitable if a high standard of decision is required. Unless the State is prepared to find all the money to pay for that high standard, the people concerned in litigation must do so. A sort of compromise has been effected in this country by the provision of Legal Aid. But a very large number of people who are not at all wealthy are nevertheless above the Legal Aid limit. They cannot afford to indulge in litigation because they cannot risk the heavy expense if they lose and sometimes the less heavy but none the less considerable expense if they win.

But even the people who are granted Legal Aid frequently have to pay quite a substantial sum towards the costs. And many of them either cannot afford or don't want to afford to spend the money. I am only talking of civil actions. In criminal cases most people charged with a serious offence can virtually get Legal Aid for nothing. This is because, although there is a provision that, if their means justify their making a contribution towards the cost or to their being refused Legal Aid, an appropriate order may be made, it is not a practical possibility for their means to be investigated sufficiently in the vast majority of cases.

But in civil cases the means of people seeking Legal Aid are carefully investigated.

The practical result is that till now most people can't afford to go to court but, when they do, they are likely to obtain a pretty reliable decision. What the Lord Chancellor is now doing for the first time in English legal history is to throw open the doors of the County Court (if the judges or registrars think fit) to anyone who is prepared to accept a fairly rough-and-ready decision. Unquestionably some such decisions will be better than decisions given according to the strict letter of the law. Palm-tree justice can sometimes be more satisfactory than the decision of the House of Lords, reached by a majority of three to two in that House and by two to one in the Court of Appeal. It is a courageous and interesting step and its success or failure will depend upon the judges and registrars who administer the new regulations. I am sure that Judges Tobin and Spencer Hogg would have been pleased if it had existed in their day.

*

I have mentioned some of the County Court judges before whom I appeared. Of course, there were many others, though altogether in the whole country there were only about fifty. I seldom appeared in a country County Court and so missed appearing before Judge Randolph, who is alleged to have had a fiery temper and to have thrown a book at somebody once.

I appeared a good many times before Judge Owen Thompson who came from the Chancery Bar, which was rather unusual. He was an extremely pleasant judge but only a moderate lawyer. On one occasion when I had become a fairly experienced practitioner in the County Court and was supposed to know a good deal about the law relating to the Rent Restriction Acts, he paid me a mild compliment. One of the rules of advocacy in this country, a rule often broken by inexperienced practitioners, is that an advocate may not tell the court what he thinks. What he must do is to make submissions. He can make as many of them as he likes, but he must not profess to be telling the judge what his own view is. His own view is irrelevant. Edward Ardizzone drew a charming illustration for my book *Brief to Counsel* of a young woman barrister addressing the court and saying: 'What I really feel in this case is –' This is not permissible, although few judges would have reprimanded a young advocate for breaking this law. Curiously enough, Ardizzone had not this in mind when he made the illustration. The picture which he drew so obviously called for the caption which I have mentioned that I inserted it.

The case before Owen Thompson involved a rather abstruse point connected with the Rent Restriction Acts. I had argued many of these cases before him but he found this a peculiarly difficult one. Eventually he said:

'I wish I could ask what you really think.'

In those days County Court judges were paid £2000 a year. In consequence, very few, if any, successful practitioners applied for the appointment. But the example of Judge Snagge shows that success at the Bar is by no means a necessary qualification for being a first-class County Court judge. Snagge had nothing of a practice at the Bar and yet, as I have said, he had all the right judicial qualities. He might well have been made a High Court judge if the first promotion from the County Court to the High Court had not been a dismal failure.

Lord Birkenhead appointed Judge Acton to be a High Court judge. Acton was an extremely well-mannered, compassionate man. He never abused his power and I would say that his sentences in criminal cases were probably just about right. But he was a very poor lawyer. 'Forever courteous and forever wrong', Keats might have written of him. He made so many mistakes of law that for a very long time successive Lord Chancellors shrank from promoting a judge from the County Court to the High Court. But the County Court gained from this reluctance and Snagge remained a splendid example of a County Court judge for many years. I have never heard anyone criticize him adversely except possibly to query whether he said too little. If that was a fault, it was certainly one on the right side and could never have been said about me.

*

The only County Court judge who was a judge when I came to the Bar and who was still a judge when I became a judge myself was Sir Gerald Hargreaves. He was a remarkable man because there were so many things he could do well. He sang, he composed, he wrote, he painted and he was a very good tennis player. He was not an erudite lawyer, but he was the personification of courtesy on the Bench. He went on playing tennis until he was a great age and then he injured a knee but did not realize the extent of the injury. The result was that he became completely crippled and for many years had to live in a chair, looked after by his devoted wife. His courage in adversity was outstanding. He died when he was about ninety, and, up to the very end of his life, he was cheerful and uncomplaining and wrote voluminous letters in entirely legible handwriting to his numerous friends.

I appeared before him a good many times and the case which I remember best was when I was against an opponent whom up to that time I had never met. It was R. C. Vaughan.

I was fairly experienced at the time and I was appearing for a landlord bringing an action for possession of a house, which was partly used as a restaurant and partly as a dwelling-house. The grounds on which the landlord was claiming possession were that the tenant was in arrear with her rent. Normally in such a case the judge would simply make an order for possession, suspended so long as the current rent was paid and something off the arrears. But there were some cases where the tenant showed that he or she was abusing the legal position and ought to be turned out. In my view this was such a case, because during the tenancy which extended over quite a number of years the tenant had almost continuously been in arrear with the rent. Letter after letter had been written to her by the landlord's solicitors and she ignored them. At least three or four sets of proceedings had been taken against her and now she was to appear again. I had little doubt that on this occasion I should be able to obtain an absolute order on behalf of my client. But I did not know R. C. Vaughan. When he started to cross-examine my client I realized that I might not have the easy victory which I anticipated. I had opened the case as that of a grossly defaulting tenant. Before Vaughan had finished his cross-examination of my client the picture was emerging of a wicked, grasping landlord, intent on harassing his wretched tenant, who was trying to eke out a living by running a small restaurant, under the continuous threat of proceedings by her landlord's solicitors.

Practitioners sometimes refer to judges as being 'landlord's judges' or 'tenant's judges'. A judge should not be either. While none of us think that we are, undoubtedly some of us have gained the reputation of being one or the other. If anything, Hargreaves was a landlord's judge. But it soon became plain that Vaughan's advocacy was making a far greater impact on the judge than were my efforts. In the end I was glad to settle the case on terms which allowed the tenant to continue in possession so long as she paid the rent and so much a week off the arrears and costs. Vaughan's advocacy was so effective that it almost made me feel ashamed to be appearing for such an unconscionable landlord, whose sole faults were that he wanted the rent which the tenant had agreed to pay, and that he gave this particular tenant more latitude than most landlords would have given. Vaughan was an exceptional advocate and, as I am unaware of any biography having been written of him, I have obtained permission from the widow of Mr Justice Elwes and from *The Times* to quote extracts from the obituary which the late judge wrote about him in that newspaper. If by the use of some Wellsian invention I could have read it before I first opposed him, I should have been more prepared for his onslaught.

R. C. Vaughan, Q.C. [wrote Mr Justice Elwes] was an unusual figure who will be greatly missed in the Temple and Gray's Inn. . . . As an advocate he was exceedingly formidable; . . . In an unpromising defence, which he always hugely enjoyed, he was at his most characteristic and not altogether easy to keep in order, denouncing impartially counsel and witnesses for the prosecution, delivering slashing attacks in all directions, and finishing up with a tremendous closing speech. Defending joint prisoners with him was like having Goliath as an ally. Nor will his supposedly inaudible current commentary be soon forgotten by those within earshot – a wider group than might have been expected . . .

Fearlessness is often praised in an advocate . . . Rex Vaughan possessed it outstandingly. When it came to the pinch he really did not care twopence for anybody . . .

That he was capable of asperity should be recorded as part of his make-up. His clients sometimes lamented his outspokenness which did not always endear him to them, lay or professional . . . Most of his brother members of the Bar . . . quickly forgave or ignored his insults, often too outrageous to be taken seriously . . .

The Temple has always had more than its share of notable characters, and among them Rex will not be soon forgotten. None of us has ever known anything quite like him. He was always twice as large as life: his successes were triumphs, his misfortunes calamities, his enemies monsters (until he relented), his friends all the salt of the earth; deafening maledictions – informed by a curious profanity – drowned his many secret kindnesses; his enmities were all fantasy, his friendships deep and true.

This note would be incomplete without a reference to his wife, who survives him and who came nearer than anybody to tempering his turbulence, and to his two small sons, whom he attempted to discipline at the top of his enormous voice as if they had been junior officers, and who were the pride and delight of his last years.

*

I did a certain number of cases in the magistrates' courts and one or two at the Old Bailey or London Sessions. My father used to tell a well-known story, no doubt apocryphal, about a man who was charged with murder and against whom the chief piece of evidence was a hat which was found near the dead body. The hat was said by the prosecution to belong to the prisoner. His counsel called evidence to show that there were thousands of these hats and accordingly, that the hat might have belonged to anybody and that certainly it was not proved that it belonged to the accused. The man was eventually acquitted and the judge told him that he was discharged. He seemed reluctant to go and eventually the judge asked him what he was waiting for.

'May I have my hat?' he asked.

I remembered this story when I was appearing for a railway-man who was charged with theft of a piece of soap and a pair of camiknickers.

The evidence was that, as he was going out of the station, the overcoat which he was carrying over his arm was searched and in it was found the soap and camiknickers. It was proved that shortly before then he had been wheeling crates containing soap and such camiknickers and that they had been broken open and a number of tablets of soap and a number of pairs of camiknickers were missing. His evidence was that he had bought the soap in a nearby market and that the camiknickers must have been put into his overcoat pocket by the real thief in the locker room where he, my client, had left it. More cami-knickers had been stolen than were found on him and more pieces of soap. It was admitted by a prosecution witness in cross-examination that the soap was of a **very** ordinary kind and sold all over the place and in particular in the market where my client said he had bought it. The accused was a man of good character and he was acquitted. The judge had obviously thought him guilty and had summed up unfavourably towards him. With my father's story in mind I could not resist applying to the judge, after the accused had been discharged, for the return of the soap. Of course, the two cases were not in *pari materia*, as in my case the defence was that the soap belonged to my client. Nevertheless, I thought they were close enough to justify me in a mild attempt to annoy the judge. I think I succeeded because he refused my application with some asperity.

❖ High Court Judges

The reputation, for good or ill, of some of the judges who were on the High Court Bench when I was called to the Bar has lasted, certainly among the legal profession. Lord Hewart was Lord Chief Justice at the time and his reputation for advocacy on the Bench is likely to remain unrivalled. I think he had the greatest command of simple English of any judge whom I've heard and it was a delight to listen to the way in which he chose his language. He had used this gift to great effect as an advocate, both in court and in the House of Commons. He was, for example, Attorney-General in 1921. At that time the editor of *John Bull*, Horatio Bottomley, was still an M.P., coming towards the end of his evil career. Prosecution was imminent, but because he was unconvicted he continued to show the Bottomley flag, to puff out his chest and to assail Ministers with questions in the House of Commons. After the 1914–18 war there were war criminals whose prosecution was contemplated. A question was asked about them on 4th August 1921 (*Hansard*, Vol. 145). The Attorney-General (Hewart) answered the question in a somewhat non-committal way. Whereupon Bottomley got up and asked in his best John Bull style:

'Is it not the intention of His Majesty's Government to prosecute these war criminals?'

To which Hewart replied: 'I entirely sympathize with the desire of the Hon. Member that criminal offenders should be punished, but I hope he will exercise a little patience.'

But Hewart's success as Attorney-General was not followed by success as Lord Chief Justice. He was a shockingly bad judge. Here is an example of his behaviour.

I had appeared at the Old Bailey for one of two defendants, and another counsel had appeared for the other. The judge at the trial, during a luncheon adjournment, promised the other counsel privately in my absence that, if his client would change his plea of not guilty to guilty, so that he could give evidence against my client, he would not send him to prison. This was, of course, a most improper procedure and my client, who was convicted, appealed on this ground. Counsel for the other accused was quite prepared to give evidence in the Court of Criminal Appeal (as it was then called) and to state what had happened between him and the judge. Lord Hewart not only refused to allow him to do this but said that nothing of the sort had happened.

Lord Hewart's was a political appointment. Up to then the Attorney-General was thought to have the moral right to be appointed Lord Chief Justice. But this tradition has now been abrogated. Moreover, few High Court judges, if any, are now appointed as a reward for political services.

*

One of the reasons why the British Bench maintains and has the reputation of maintaining a very high standard of integrity is the intimacy which exists among judges and barristers. Every barrister who has achieved a sufficient measure of success to be considered for appointment to the Bench is well known to most of his colleagues and to most of the judges. The Bar has a very high standard of integrity. There are, however, not only a very few black sheep, that is people who would be disbarred if the truth were known about them, but there are also a few practitioners who do not reach the standard of integrity which would be required of them on the Bench. The expression which is sometimes used of such people is that you have to 'watch' them. This sort of thing is known to the Lord Chancellor and those members of the profession whom he consults. In consequence, no barrister, however successful, who has to be 'watched', is ever appointed. In the result the standard of integrity of the Bench is never impaired.

It is true that some appointments are made of able and trustworthy advocates, who are unsuited to the judicial life. Sometimes, if an appointment is bad, it is because the new judge abuses his power. In his own court a judge wields so much power and outside it he is subject to so much adulation and flattery that a few judges are unable to resist the temptation which this power gives them. Such appointments are fortunately rare and they would be rarer still if every judge had to do a probationary period of two or three months and if before that he were warned by a really good, experienced judge about the dangers of abuse of power. I am sure that I should have been a better judge, certainly in my first years, if I had had some good advice from an experienced colleague before I tried my first case.

I do not think that the advantage to the country of a Bench of the highest integrity and wholly unaffected by political considerations can be exaggerated. When I was appointed to be a judge in 1949 there were not more than a hundred judges altogether, including those in the House of Lords and the judges of County Courts. Today there are about four hundred. The number is becoming dangerously large. It is to be hoped that the Royal Commission under Lord Pearson which is considering, among other things, the trial of road accident cases, will recommend that the trial of liability in these cases should be abolished and a form of national insurance take its place. Should this happen, the judges will be relieved of a substantial quantity of work and the continuous addition to their ranks, which has been a feature of the legal profession since the Courts Act 1971 came into force, will slow down and, it is to be hoped, stop.

*

Three of the best-known of the King's Bench judges in the years 1920–30 were Avory, Swift and McCardie.

Avory was a very small man with a parchment-like face and a rather rasping Cockney accent. He was quite a good criminal lawyer but nothing like as good as his reputation supposed him to be. This reputation sprang from the fact that the standard of lawyer at the Criminal Bar was not high and that Avory was far above it. He was a stern judge, but would decide a point of law quite dispassionately and would not attempt to twist the law to the disadvantage of the prisoner.

I sometimes used to drive behind him in the park when I was going to the Temple. He went in a chauffeur-driven car and the chauffeur obviously had strict orders not to exceed the twenty miles an hour speed limit which then existed. Although his parchment-like face suggested that he was never swayed by emotion, this was not so and he did occasionally lose his temper and his anger was reproduced in his sentence. For example, in what was called the *Stella Maris* case a man named Alphonso Smith was charged with the murder of a man called Derham, who had been having an affair with Mrs Smith while her husband was away at the war. Alphonso Smith was alleged to have shot her lover. His defence was that he was so upset when he came home on leave and found what had happened between his wife and Derham, that he decided to commit suicide and for this purpose he loaded his service revolver. He was walking along the road and he happened to meet Derham. They got into a heated conversation which resulted in some violence and somehow or other the revolver came out and somehow or other it went off and Derham died in consequence.

Roland Oliver was prosecuting and Marshall Hall defending. Marshall Hall was quite prepared to advise his client to plead guilty to manslaughter and Roland Oliver was quite prepared to accept this plea on behalf of the prosecution. He realized that the sympathy of the jury would be with the man in the dock, who, while serving his country, found that Derham had been seducing his wife. But Avory refused to agree to this suggestion. Had Alphonso Smith pleaded guilty to manslaughter, he could have been sentenced to a good many years of imprisonment and justice would probably have been done.

However, as it turned out, the jury acquitted Alphonso Smith both of murder and manslaughter. Roland Oliver, appreciating this possibility, had inserted another charge against him, namely that of carrying firearms with intent to endanger life. After his acquittal on the two main charges, Marshall Hall asked the judge whether in his view, if a man were carrying a loaded revolver with intent to kill himself, that constituted the offence of carrying firearms with intent to endanger life. Avory said that in his view it did. Marshall Hall accordingly advised his client to plead guilty to that charge.

In those days it was an offence to attempt to commit suicide, but when people were charged with this offence, they were only sent to prison if it was thought that this would be in their own interest. Alphonso Smith had not gone as far as attempting suicide. He was merely carrying about with him the means by which he could commit suicide. In other words, his offence was less than that of attempted suicide. Avory sentenced him to a year's imprisonment with hard labour. Such an unfair sentence could only have been due to the judge's anger at the verdict of acquittal. It was a most improper sentence but Alphonso Smith did not appeal, no doubt being delighted with the verdict of the jury on the other charges and realizing that, if the judge had accepted counsel's suggestion, he would have been sent to prison for some years. In those circumstances one year seemed almost like a birthday present.

Swift was a remarkable character and, although he was a poor lawyer and not a good judge, he was personally very popular. He was very much in command of his own court and no one could take liberties with him. He would almost always try to find in favour of a man who had been seriously injured in an accident. He had a splendidly imitable North Country accent and the stories about him are legion. He was a pleasant enough judge to appear before, but it was very difficult to penetrate his mind after lunch. It would have been a great loss to the Bench if Swift had never become a judge, because he was warm-hearted, he had a great sense of fun and, in spite of his limitations, he was a judicial giant.

C

McCardie was a charming judge and an excellent judge of fact. He probably had more knowledge of case law than any other judge on the Bench, but he did not always know how to apply it. His judgments usually contained a reference to most of the cases on the subject which had preceded it. His public quarrel with Lord Justice Scrutton and his suicide and the reasons for it have been told by others. I only have happy recollections of appearing before him.

*

Mr Justice Macnaghten, affectionately known to practitioners as 'Muggins', was the son of a famous judge, Lord Macnaghten. (Some people still think that one or other of them had something to do with the McNaughton Rules. Although the McNaughton of the Rules has had his name spelled in many different ways, he was not a judge, not even a lawyer. He was a man who was charged with murder and whose defence was insanity. The judges were asked to formulate the Common Law rules relating to insanity as a defence. This was in 1843 and at that time and until 1883 criminals, who successfully raised the defence of insanity, were found not guilty on that ground. But in 1883, after a man had taken a pot-shot at Queen Victoria, she was incensed with the idea that he could be found not guilty.

'Not guilty!' she said. 'I saw him do it.'

So in 1883 the verdict was changed to 'Guilty but insane', the full verdict being 'Guilty of the act charged but so insane at the time as not to be responsible in law for it'. But in 1964 Parliament changed the law again and said that such a man was to be found 'Not guilty by reason of insanity'. Elizabeth II had no objection, though the shade of Queen Victoria might have said, when complaining at her successor's assenting to the change:

'If someone had shot at you, you might have thought differently.' But I am sure that Queen Victoria's shade would have been wrong.)

Muggins was not a great judge like his father, but what a lot of people, even in the legal profession, did not know was that he had a great sense of humour, one of the differences between him and the famous judicial jester, Mr Justice Darling, being that Muggins kept his wit for his chambers and his friends, while Mr Justice Darling frequently paraded it for the benefit of the Press. But though a sense of humour may go with an erudite knowledge of the law, it was not so in the case of Mr Justice Macnaghten. He was made a judge in the days when unfortunately Lord Chancellors were wont to reward well-behaved Members of Parliament with High Court judgeships. Muggins had been for many years the member for Londonderry, and he became a judge in 1925. I appeared before him on a good number of occasions. He was pleasant enough and did not throw his weight about or otherwise abuse his power. But I am afraid that his nickname was fairly earned. Moreover, his standard of morality was so high that he was quite unable to understand or tolerate the behaviour of those who did not come up to it.

I once had a case before him where a man and woman, who had been living together, had fallen out and were suing each other. I do not remember the facts of the case but I do remember that there was acute conflict of evidence and I had submitted to Muggins that he should believe my client. Whereupon he said:

'How can I believe either of these parties? They have admitted living together when they were not married.'

My suggestion that, because a man was sexually immoral, he was not necessarily a liar, was not acceded to.

Mr Justice Darling was made a peer (not a law lord) in 1924 but he often came to sit as additional judge in the King's Bench Division after his elevation. I should like to make some amends to his memory for something which I wrote in a book called *Tipping the Scales*. I then said that he, with three other judges, were four of the worst judges of the twentieth century. No one disagreed with me about the other three judges, but several judges and barristers whose experience of the judge was greater than mine have told me that Mr Justice Darling was not at all a bad criminal judge, even though he was incapable of restraining Mr Pemberton Billing when he was charged with criminal libel at the Old Bailey. Henry Dickens was one of those who stood up for him.

Darling used to sit in King's Bench Court IV, which was in consequence always well attended by the Press. Although he often used his wit for the pleasure of reading about it at breakfast in the morning papers, this was not always his purpose. For example, he tried a case in which a clergyman was claiming damages for fraud for being tricked into buying some worthless shares by a door-to-door salesman, who in those days was allowed to peddle stocks and shares as though they were vacuum cleaners. The case was tried before Mr Justice Darling, sitting with a jury. Counsel for the defendants, in his final speech to the jury, dwelt upon the fact that the law of this country is *caveat emptor* – let the buyer beware. A vendor of goods, he said, was not bound to disparage the goods he wanted to sell. He was under no obligation to cry 'stinking fish'. In his summing-up the judge said words to this effect: 'Counsel for the defendant has very properly told you, members of the jury, that it is no part of the law of England that a man who is selling goods has got to say harsh things about them. He is quite right. A fishmonger,' said the judge, 'is under no obligation to cry "stinking fish, stinking fish", but,' he went on, 'if he knows that his fish do stink he is not entitled to cry falsely "fresh fish, fresh fish", nor is he any the more entitled to do that *if he happens to know that his customer cannot smell.*'

Another King's Bench judge worth mentioning is Mr Justice Horridge. He was quite a good judge, though a little on the stern side. Young advocates found him rather intimidating. Some witnesses also found him a little difficult, though at first they were disarmed by what appeared to be the kindly smile with which he looked at them. Sometimes a rather bumptious witness, encouraged by his smile, would try to crack a joke. The judge jumped on him immediately, and the poor fellow couldn't think what he had done to change the benevolent and encouraging-looking judge into what appeared to him to be a judicial monster. The solution was quite simple. Half of Mr

Justice Horridge's face was paralysed and made him look as though he were smiling. It was rather bad luck on the witness.

'How do you make your living?' asked Horridge.

'The same as you do, my Lord. My job depends upon the stupidity of the public, so we are in the same boat, eh, my Lord?'

'Behave yourself,' said Horridge. 'Stand up and take your hands out of your pockets and don't try to be funny.'

Many years later, when I was a judge, I was talking to a newly appointed colleague about the judicial treatment of witnesses. I said how important it was for a judge, as far as possible, to put a witness at his ease and not to let him feel that he was disbelieved for some reason extraneous to the merits of the case, for example by blundering over the oath or by not being respectful enough to the judge.

'For that reason,' I said, perhaps rather too complacently, 'I never tell a witness who has his hands in his pockets to take them out. Otherwise, if he lost the case, he might think that he had lost it for that reason.'

To which my colleague rejoined: 'So the poor fellow never learns why he lost the case.'

Horridge also had a high standard of morality, in spite of the fact that for some time he was lent to the Divorce Court and became acquainted with a good deal of sexual immorality at second hand. His standard of general morality can be gauged by the following incident. Counsel had referred to a man giving a post-dated cheque and said:

'There's nothing in that, my Lord.'

'I hope I've never given one,' said Horridge.

The standard of lawyer among Chancery judges is normally higher than that among the Common Law judges. There are, of course, exceptions, like the obvious one of Lord Atkin. It must have been a great pleasure to appear before him when he was a puisne judge, but I never had the opportunity because he was already in the Court of Appeal when I came to the Bar. But an exception the other way round was that of Mr Justice Eve. He was a robust Chancery judge whose behaviour was much more that of a King's Bench judge, and he was quite a good judge of fact. But he was not a good lawyer. And it was perhaps a little unfortunate that occasionally he was asked to sit in the Court of Appeal.

The following episode, which I believe took place in his court, though I am not certain of it, had nothing to do with his competence as a lawyer.

I remember counsel for one side or the other addressing the judge in his final speech and eventually he said, 'My Lord, I don't want to gild the lily but –' and then he went on to emphasize the many points that there were in his favour. As he said 'to gild the lily' I noticed a thoughtful expression come over the judge's face. This continued during the next five minutes. Counsel obviously imagined that the judge had been listening intently to his argument and that he was making some impression on him, but at the end of five minutes the judge said:

'Mr So-and-so, isn't it "to paint the lily, to gild refined gold"?' This was a good example of the dangers of misquotation. Counsel had lost the ear of the judge for a full five minutes.

A King's Bench judge before whom I liked to appear, although he was a really bad judge, was Mr Justice Charles. He was very breezy and cheerful and no lawyer at all. He was a bad judge of fact, and, worse than that, he would often form a view of the case much too early and try to run the case from that time on against the party who, in his belief, was in the wrong. Advocates who knew of this weakness on the part of the judge would take advantage of it. If Charles jumped against you very early on in a case the thing to do was not to complain about it or even to enter into mild argument with him, but to let him have his head completely until you could produce some very strong point in favour of your client. The result of doing this would often be that Charles would turn round and pursue the man in whose favour he had originally been, as though he were an unmitigated villain.

I once had an enticement case before Charles in which a bank clerk was suing a film producer for damages for enticing his wife. Although enticement cases were not popular with judges, this did seem as though it might be a real example of a morally unscrupulous film producer enticing by the glamour of the film world an attractive girl, who was tired of the humdrum life of a bank clerk's wife. Charles early on in the case took this view and it became obvious while I was cross-examining the plaintiff. But unfortunately for him the plaintiff's legal advisers had put their case much too high and charged my client with wholesale adultery with the woman in question. They failed to prove any act of adultery at all. In those days adultery was looked upon as a very serious matter and Charles was horrified by what appeared to be the wholly unfounded allegations made against my client. He proceeded to go into reverse.

It's a curious fact that, when one thing starts to go wrong with a case, a lot of other things start to go wrong too. In their efforts to prove adultery against my client the plaintiff's advisers had employed a private detective who, when my client was visiting the plaintiff's wife during the day and had his car outside her flat – she was then living apart from her husband – thought it a good idea to remove the ignition key from the car. In those days people often did not lock their cars and left the ignition keys in them. My client very sensibly rang up his solicitors when he discovered what had happened and told them that he would have to leave his car all night outside the lady's residence. They took the necessary action by writing to the plaintiff's solicitors. Not only therefore did this evidence come to nothing, but while I was cross-examining the detective in question I was suddenly told by my solicitor client that there was a police officer in court who had informed him that this detective had twice been convicted in a magistrates' court of making a false declaration, an offence akin to perjury.

When I am giving advice to newly called barristers I some-times quote this case to them as a useful lesson. There was no time to investigate whether what the police officer said was accurate or not and, if I had put those matters to the witness and he had denied them, the judge might well have been so angry at unfounded allegations of that kind being made against a witness that he would have turned round yet again and run the case in favour of the plaintiff. On the other hand, if the allegations were true, they would be extremely useful to my client's case. One should never put a grave allegation to a witness unless one has substantial evidence to support it. In the case of an alleged conviction one should usually have a certified copy of the conviction, for without it there can be no certainty. So I had to wait my opportunity. It came when the witness asked me if I would explain a question. I said, 'I'm so sorry. It's my fault. I realize how difficult it is to give evidence. I don't suppose you've ever been in court before.' If he had said no, he hadn't, I would have left the matter there, but he said nothing, so I said, 'That's right, isn't it? You've never been in court before?' He didn't answer.

'Well, have you?' I said.

Eventually he said: 'Yes.'

I could tell from his reluctance to answer the question in the affirmative that the information which I had been given was in all probability true. Nevertheless it was necessary to proceed with the greatest caution.

'I suppose you were giving evidence in an accident case or something like that?' I said.

'No,' he said.

'What sort of a court was it in?' I asked. 'A County Court?'

'A police court,' he said.

'You were a witness, I suppose?' I asked.

He didn't answer.

'Well, were you?'

'No,' he said.

'You were prosecuting someone then?' I asked.

He hesitated and then said: 'No.'

'Well, what were you doing there?'

'I was a defendant,' he said reluctantly.

'A motoring offence, I suppose?' I asked.

'No,' he said.

'Well, what was it?'

'I was charged with making a false declaration,' he said.

'Did you plead guilty or not guilty?'

'Guilty.'

'And that was the only time you've ever been in court before?'

'No, there was one other occasion.'

'In what court?'

'A police court.'

'And what was the reason for that?'

'I was again charged with making a false declaration.'

'Did you plead guilty or not guilty?'

'Guilty.'

After this, nothing could hold Mr Justice Charles. And when my client went into the witness-box and was cross-examined by opposing counsel, Charles stood over him like a mother hen protecting her chicks.

'Did you make a will in favour of my client's wife?' asked counsel.

'Yes, I did.'

'Very proper,' said Charles.

*

It is a great advantage for a practitioner to know his judge. Some of them have idiosyncracies. Mr Justice Wynn-Parry, for example, publicly rebuked a barrister for appearing before him when not wearing a waistcoat. A more courteous way of administering this rebuke would have been to send a note to the offending party to ask him to wear a waistcoat in future.

I had rather a bad habit of swaying from side to side and on one occasion it infuriated Mr Justice Talbot. Eventually he could stand it no longer.

'For heaven's sake, don't sway from side to side,' he said.

No judge is going to decide against a litigant because his counsel doesn't wear a waistcoat or sways from side to side, but if the case starts with counsel being rebuked in that manner and counsel is not very experienced, the result may be that the advocate will consciously or unconsciously be sufficiently upset that he will not do his case justice when he presents it. I therefore used to advise my pupils of any particular foibles which I knew certain judges to have and I advised them always to know how to pronounce judges' names. I am sure that there are still some practitioners who pronounce the name of Mr Justice Lopes to rhyme with ropes, which they wouldn't dream of doing if it were spelled with a 'z' at the end instead of an 's'.

Most judges have a judicial sense and, even if they are not great lawyers or even good judges of fact, they do understand how essential it is that both parties should feel that they have had a fair trial, even though the losing party may resent the judgment. Mr Justice Hilbery was a junior when I came to the Bar, but after the war I appeared before him when he was a High Court judge. I was acting for a boy who had fallen over a bath in the school playground. It was not an easy case and, as Hilbery had the reputation of being a defendant's judge, he would not have been a good judge to try this case from my client's point of view. During some preliminary application about the case Hilbery made some jocular remark like: 'Who had a bath, did you say?' A day or two later, when the case was about to come on before Hilbery, he sent for me and my opponent and spoke to us privately. This is what he said:

'Isn't this the case,' he asked, 'where I made some remark which the plaintiff might have thought was disparaging his case? It was about a bath, I think.'

I said that it was that case.

'Well,' said Hilbery, 'would your client prefer this case to be tried before another judge?'

I said that quite frankly we would, and accordingly the case was transferred to the list of Mr Justice Stable, who was a much better tribunal from our point of view. We lost the case, just the same, but Hilbery's conduct was a good example of judicial behaviour on the English Bench.

⊞ Judicial Test Teams

When I came to the Bar in 1923 there were sixteen judges who normally sat in the King's Bench Division, including the Lord Chief Justice, and there were two Probate, Divorce and Admiralty judges. There are now forty-one Queen's Bench judges, the Lord Chief Justice, and eighteen Family Division judges. Since 1971 the Probate, Divorce and Admiralty Division has ceased to exist. Contested cases about wills have gone to the Chancery Division, and Admiralty cases have gone to the Queen's Bench Division. Matrimonial cases and cases concerning infants in the High Court are heard in the new Family Division.

I have only appeared before two Lord Chief Justices, Lord Hewart and Lord Goddard. During the war Lord Caldecote took the place of Lord Hewart, who retired for health reasons. Lord Caldecote was by all accounts a pleasant enough but not very effectual Lord Chief Justice, and, if one can judge by reports of cases which he decided, he was certainly not a profound lawyer.

I have previously referred to Lord Hewart. There are three things to be said in his favour as a judge. I have already mentioned his wonderful command of simple English. But, much more important, in most cases his only object was to procure what he considered to be a just decision, even though his opinion might be wrong and his method of giving effect to it deplorable. He was also quite a good lawyer.

Lord Goddard was, in my view rightly, considered to be a great Lord Chief Justice. But like other great men he had defects. He was too impatient and in his latter years, in order to relieve his feelings, he would carry on a *sotto voce* monologue (not always so *sotto*) with such expressions as: 'Why doesn't the fellow get on with it', 'He's said that before', 'Can't hear a word he's saying', 'What on earth has that to do with it?' And so on.

In 1971 I delivered the Hamlyn lectures in the Hall at Gray's Inn. Lord Goddard, although he was old and ill and in a wheelchair, came to the first of them. I must say that I was very surprised and gratified. His hearing was by then very bad indeed. He was sitting on the platform a few places away from me in his wheelchair and for the first five minutes my lecture was punctuated by a stream of fairly loud whispers from Goddard: 'What's the fellow saying? Can't hear a word he says. What? Why can't he speak up?' But at the end of five minutes I am glad to say that I had lulled him to sleep.

Although Lord Goddard was a strong judge, he was not an obstinate one. But, of course, he made mistakes sometimes. One of them was to interfere with the method of summing-up in criminal cases. Most people have heard the expression 'beyond all reasonable doubt'. It used to be the way in which all judges summed up to juries in criminal cases.

'Members of the jury,' they would say, 'before you can convict the prisoner of this crime you must be satisfied of his guilt beyond all reasonable doubt.'

But few people outside the legal profession know that after Lord Goddard became Lord Chief Justice he began to interfere with this method of summing-up. Indeed, in one case it appeared that he was telling other judges that they should not use the expression at all. His reason for doing this was because in the past some judges tried to explain to jurymen what a reasonable doubt meant. They did not always do it very well. Lord Goddard thought such explanations might confuse jurymen rather than assist them. The sort of explanation which used to be given was this.

'Now what do I mean by a reasonable doubt, members of the

jury? It means simply this. In your own personal affairs you may have to make an important decision which might affect you for the rest of your life and whether you decided this way or that might depend upon the existence of certain facts, which you did not know for certain of your own knowledge. You had only heard the information from other people. Was it true? If it was true, you would make an affirmative decision. Well, now, members of the jury, if you were sufficiently satisfied of its truth to act upon it and to make that affirmative decision then you would be satisfied beyond all reasonable doubt. I hope I have made myself clear.'

Few lawyers would criticize Lord Goddard for saying that such an explanation might in fact confuse the jurors. On the other hand, if no explanation is given, jurors as a whole for many, many years seem to have appreciated that what was implied by the expression was that, before you can convict a man of crime, a very high measure of proof was required. It certainly appears that, if Lord Goddard had not interfered, judges and jurors would have carried on as before and that no one would have been any the worse off. However, Lord Goddard at first told the judges that what they must say was that the jury must be sure or feel sure of the prisoner's guilt before they could convict him. For some time after this pronouncement judges simply did not know how to sum up and, in consequence, one judge summed up too uncertainly in a murder case and the Court of Criminal Appeal (as it was then called) had to quash the conviction against a man.

After that, Lord Goddard slightly modified his view and many judges today try to combine the old direction with Lord Goddard's views. 'Members of the jury,' they will say, 'if you feel sure of the prisoner's guilt beyond all reasonable doubt', or 'Members of the jury, you must be satisfied beyond all reasonable doubt that you are sure of the prisoner's guilt' or 'Members of the jury, you must feel sure that you are satisfied beyond all reasonable doubt'.

Everyone makes mistakes and my belief that this was one of Lord Goddard's in no way lessens my admiration for him as a judge. But what does 'feel sure' or 'be sure' mean? Supposing after a judge had summed up to a jury in these words: 'Members of the jury, you must feel sure of the prisoner's guilt', a juryman got up and said, 'My Lord, might I ask your Lordship a question?' 'What is it?' 'Well, what exactly does your Lordship mean by "feel sure"?' The judge might reply, possibly a little testily: 'What do I mean by "feel sure"? I mean you've got to feel quite sure, of course. I should have thought that was obvious.' 'Well, my Lord,' the juryman might go on, 'I feel quite sure that I can see your Lordship. Have I got to be as sure as that?' 'Of course not.' 'Now your Lordship seems to be saying that I've got to be not quite sure.'

Those were fair questions by the juryman and they demonstrate the difficulty of explaining what 'sure' means. Sometimes it means that the person who uses the expression is very far from sure. 'I'm sure I brought it with me,' he says, feeling in his pocket feverishly and strongly suspecting that he left it at home.

It would in my view have been far better if Lord Goddard had left judges to sum up as they had in the past, and often when I went to legal gatherings, and was called upon to speak, I referred to the matter and would start off a speech with such words as 'if I were sure' or something of that kind and then play about with the expressions 'sure', 'nearly sure', 'almost sure' and 'quite sure' and finally 'beyond all reasonable doubt'.

Some years ago my wife and I were driving to a legal dinner where I had promised to speak for about ten minutes.

'What shall I talk about?' I asked rhetorically. 'I know. I'll give them the "be sure and beyond all reasonable doubt" stuff.'

My wife had heard me talk on this subject all too often with an enthusiasm which she did not share and at what was, from her point of view and probably other people's, inordinate length. So, after a sigh, she said:

'D'you know, when you're dead, I'm going to put upon your tombstone – "Gone beyond all reasonable doubt".'

I was most grateful to her for this and I used it to end my speech that evening with great effect, although I am afraid

that few people gave my wife the credit for making the remark
and thought that I had invented it. Since that evening I have
used it over and over again to end a speech and my unfortunate
wife has heard it far more often than she used to hear the 'be
sure and beyond all reasonable doubt' stuff.

*

Most of the High Court judges before whom I appeared in the
twenties and thirties were good judges. But Mr Justice Fraser,
though a good judge, was not fitted by temperament to be one.
He worried so much about his cases that about two years after
his appointment he died. With the exception of Lord Hewart
and Mr Justice Shearman, they were all pleasant to appear
before. But one had to know Mr Justice Bailhache. He had a
very quick mind and had little difficulty in making it up. He
was usually right. But the inexperienced practitioner who did
not know him and who sought to make a long speech on a
question of fact at the end of a case would find himself cut short.
  'You don't want to address me on the facts, I imagine,' he
would say.
  'Well, my Lord –'
  'I've made up my mind.'
  'But, my Lord –'
  'There's no law in the case, is there?'
  'No, my Lord, it's purely a question of fact.'
  'Well, I'm against you.'
  'But, my Lord –'
  'You can go to the Court of Appeal if you think I'm wrong.'
And that was normally the end of that.
  Mr Justice Rowlatt was a good judge and an extremely
nice one, but he was rather nervous. This was betrayed by the
fact that he often played about with a handkerchief over his
face and would sometimes give rather nervous laughs. This was
a little unsettling for a prisoner whom he was about to sentence
to a long term of penal servitude. His semi-laughs and nervous
manner created a false impression of what was going on in his
mind, even though the words he used were plain enough.

'You're a very wicked man,' he would say, as he tried with his handkerchief to hide his nervous laugh, 'and you'll go to penal servitude for ten years.' His manner, though not his words, was more in keeping with an invitation to tea after the case was over.

Mr Justice Salter was a judge who seldom smiled. In court he was probably the driest of all the judges. But he had a sense of humour and it was, I think, during an after-dinner speech that he said: 'When I was at the Bar it seemed to me that judges had very thick heads and one might have to say a thing two, three or four times before one could get one's argument across. But now I am on the Bench I can't understand why counsel repeat themselves so often.'

This reminds me of what Lord Justice Scrutton said about me in his not altogether unkindly judgment, after I had addressed the Court of Appeal in my very early days at the Bar.

'I will only say this to him,' he said, 'that he's not very trustful of the court, for, having said a thing three times, he goes on to repeat it a fourth.'

*

I hope that it does not appear too arrogant for someone who never became more than a County Court judge to attempt to assess the merits and qualities of judges of a much higher rank. I fully appreciate that some or all of my views may not be shared by lawyers better qualified to express an opinion. But I thought it possible that it might be of a little interest to state my views, if only because it would help lawyers who knew the judges in question in coming to a conclusion about me. And, if I am guilty of the offence of arrogance, I cannot resist the temptation of making it worse by preparing lists of two judicial test teams of judges who functioned during the last fifty years. But only those who are dead qualify for inclusion. It would be invidious to refer to any judge who is still alive, in whichever eleven he would have been included.

In the first eleven are the top-class lawyers. In the second eleven are the best judges of first instance. The first-class lawyer is not necessarily a first-class judge, and vice versa. A good example of a first-class judge who was not a great lawyer is Mr Justice Geoffrey Lawrence (subsequently Lord Oaksey). It was an excellent appointment to make him President at Nuremberg. He was patient, courteous, quiet, understanding and percipient. He was therefore an outstandingly good judge of first instance but it is most improbable that he would ever have become a law lord except for the fact that he presided so well at the Nuremberg trials. I make him captain of the second eleven, though Finlay ran him close and was a better lawyer. In some ways Lynskey was better than either of them. But, although all three judges were compassionate, Lynskey rather lacked the *appearance* of compassion which both the other judges exhibited.

Not surprisingly all the best lawyers became law lords. I have put the teams in alphabetical order:

1st Eleven	*2nd Eleven*
Lords Atkin (captain)	Justices[1] Asquith
Dunedin (vice-captain)	Birkett
Du Parcq	Finlay (vice-captain)
Goddard	Greer
Jenkins	Lawrence (Lord Oaksey) (captain)
Porter	Lynskey
Russell	McCardie
Simonds	Parker
Sumner	Roche
Tomlin	Sankey
Uthwatt	Tucker

I was tempted to make a third eleven of the worst judges, but, while I think it's fair to express my views about individual judges who were on the Bench when I practised, it might be unnecessarily hurtful to relatives and descendants of deceased

---

[1] The plural of 'Mr Justice' is 'Justices', a fact which may be rather confusing to the layman, who thinks that the word 'Justices' means JPs. It usually does.

judges to categorize as many as eleven of them in a highly adverse manner just because in my opinion they fall into that category. I therefore resisted the temptation.

So, intead of making a worst eleven, I will refer to a letter of congratulation which I wrote to a friend of mine on his appointment to the High Court Bench. I happened to meet him just after his appointment and, having congratulated him, I said that this meeting would save me the trouble of writing a letter.

'Not a bit of it,' he said. 'I should like to know how you put it.'

So I wrote the following letter.

Barbara and I were delighted to read of your appointment and we send you our hearty congratulations. I was glad to anticipate this letter by giving you my best wishes in person, but I'm afraid that, if you expect the sort of letter Charles Lamb might have included in an essay 'On Congratulating a Judge on his Appointment', you will be sadly disappointed. You want someone like Richard Elwes to do that. Did you ever read his wonderful obituary of Rex Vaughan? You see how right I was. I am already talking about obituaries. Yet perhaps it would be no bad way to write to a newly appointed judge something on these lines.

'I hope that in the end it will be said of you that he was courteous, quick-minded, patient, tolerant and a sound lawyer.'

I feel quite sure that something of this kind and many other good things will be said of you, but I hope that I never see them.

🎴 In Practice

In my first year at the Bar I was paid (I won't say I earned) thirty-eight guineas. (But I did not give it to my father, who had paid my pupillage fee.) In my second year I was more successful and was paid forty-one guineas. In my third year it was 150 guineas, in my fourth 200 and in my fifth 400. It was not until my sixth year, when my income was about 800 guineas, that I could be said to have acquired some kind of practice. Although 800 guineas was worth very much more than it is now, even allowing for the decrease in the value of money it is certainly less than a successful practitioner of six years' standing would earn today. By 1949, when I became a judge, I was earning £7000 a year.

After five years in Fortune's chambers I decided to move. Fortune was then extremely busy and the clerk had to devote most of his time to looking after him. In addition to that, Dickens had his medical practice and Sir Alfred Callaghan was still around doing County Court cases or getting me to do them for him. I did quite a lot of devilling for other people outside chambers. Sometimes I was paid for this and sometimes I was not, but there is no doubt whatever that it would have been worth my while, if I had had the means, to offer to pay to be allowed to do the work.

Among those for whom I devilled were Walter Frampton (father of the present Walter Frampton whom I always look

upon as 'young Walter', although I think that he has already
retired from being a Metropolitan magistrate), N. R. Fox-
Andrews, B. L. O'Malley and a few others.

Having acquired a small practice, I wanted to find chambers
where there was a clerk who could devote more time towards
nursing and increasing it. So I went into the chambers of C. T.
Le Quesne, K.C., where there was only one junior barrister,
Frank Gahan. In Fortune's chambers I had only had to pay
£65 a year altogether for the share of a small room and the
services of the clerk. I had to pay over double this when I went
into Le Quesne's chambers, but I considered it well worth it.

Le Quesne was extremely nice to me and I always got along
with him very well. He was a very fine lawyer and was at the
Commercial Bar, where the standard of lawyer is high. He had
had a huge practice as a junior and before he took silk he must
have been making at least between £5000 and £10,000 a year.
Such an income in those days was very large indeed.

He had taken silk before I came to his chambers but he did
not make a success of it. This was for two reasons. Although his
legal knowledge and his ability to understand difficult legal
points and to apply the law to complicated facts were really
second to no one's at the Commercial Bar, he was only an
average advocate and he was rather too inclined to assume that
he had sufficiently made a point when he had stated it once in
clear terms.

To some extent his methods were the opposite of Fortune's.
Whereas Le Quesne would sometimes fail to press a good point
of law hard enough, Fortune would be likely to press a bad
point of law too hard. As a junior, Le Quesne's advocacy was
sufficient, because in a large action he would always be led by
a silk. But it was essential that as a silk he should be a first-class
advocate and he failed in this respect.

A minor reason, also, for his failure as a silk was his insistence
upon having too many consultations with his clients. Solicitors
got tired of being summoned to his chambers so often. He would
have innumerable consultations in a case and they would not
only be large in number but protracted in time. Solicitors and

their managing clerks became tired of this and they nicknamed him 'King Con'.

But although his practice gradually declined, it did not do so before he had appeared in a number of important cases. I suppose the biggest of all was *The Bank of Portugal* v. *Waterlow*.

The printers William Waterlow & Son used to print the bank-notes for the Bank of Portugal. A Dutch crook named Marang (he might well have been called a King Con man) approached Sir William Waterlow in London privately, persuaded him that he had the authority of the Portuguese Government and arranged with him to have printed a large number of notes for Portugal's colony Angola. Marang told Sir William that there were important political reasons why this should be kept entirely confidential, and he told him that an arrangement for the distribution of the notes would be made through Waterlow's agent in Angola. He said that an authorized representative of the Bank of Portugal would call on the agent for the purpose of making these arrangements. When Waterlow wrote confidentially to his agent in Angola telling him about the matter, the agent wrote a letter to him warning him to take great precautions to see that everything was in order and adding that there were more things happening in Angola than he dared mention. To this letter Waterlow telegraphed what in our chambers became a catch-phrase: 'Do nothing say nothing wait for the call of the gentleman.' Even now I still find it somewhat irresistible.

Everyone accepted Sir William Waterlow's good faith. It is still a mystery how a man in his position could have acted with such incredible stupidity.

The notes were duly printed and delivered to the conspirators, who at once started a bank to dispose of them. It was some little time before the fraud was discovered and then the Bank of Portugal had to call in the forged notes and pay for them as though they were genuine. They claimed damages against Waterlow's for the cost of doing this.

The case illustrated the uncertainties and expense of the law. It was originally heard by the then Mr Justice Wright, who

awarded the Bank of Portugal substantial damages. Waterlow
& Son appealed and the Court of Appeal somewhat reduced
the damages but otherwise dismissed the appeal. But this decision was by a majority of the court only. The third judge, Lord
Justice Scrutton, held that as the Bank of Portugal only had to
print more money to replace the forged bank-notes which had
to be called in, their only real loss was the extra cost of printing.
And he would have reduced the damages to that amount, which
was trifling. Both sides appealed to the House of Lords, who, by
a majority of 3 to 2, gave the Bank of Portugal more damages
than Mr Justice Wright had ordered. But the two dissenting
members of the House agreed with Lord Justice Scrutton. That
was a close thing, but at any rate in that case six judges rejected
the 'paper for paper' argument, as against three who thought
that argument should succeed.

But a far more unsatisfactory case took place many years
later when Mr Onassis and Mme Callas sued Mr Vergottis. In
that case the judge who tried the case found in favour of
Mr Onassis and Mme Callas. Mr Vergottis appealed and the
Court of Appeal unanimously found in his favour. Thereupon
Mr Onassis and Mme Callas appealed to the House of Lords
who, by a majority of 3 to 2, reversed the decision of the Court
of Appeal and found in favour of the plaintiffs. In the result,
although five superior court judges found in Mr Vergottis's
favour and only four against him, he ended up the loser.

Our present system of law, on the whole, works extremely
well but there is bound to be an occasional case like that of
Mr Vergottis, where the losing party must think it a very odd
system.

*

It was between my move to Le Quesne's chambers in 1929 and
the beginning of the 1939–45 war that I gradually built up my
practice. Before the war started I had given up quite a large
County Court practice and appeared mainly in what was then
the King's Bench Division. I also went into the Chancery
Division, the Bankruptcy Court and what was then the Probate,

Divorce and Admiralty Division. Occasionally I did a criminal case.

A busy junior works more hours than most people in other professions. People vary as to how they find these hours. Some of them get up very early in the morning and some of them go to bed very late. I went to bed very late and occasionally had to work right through the night. I learned from experience that, although one might be tired during a case, it was vital to know every aspect of it thoroughly. I also found it a great help (and indeed essential) to commit everything to paper. Before I went into court I would have a note for the examination of every witness whom I was calling and for the cross-examination of every witness whom I expected the other side to call. The notes would be in a very short form, but, as far as I could make them, they would be comprehensive. Each note would be sufficient to bring to my mind the subject-matter about which I wanted to question the witness, e.g. 'letter, page 54; visit to the zoo, etc.' I know that some barristers have advised young men not to rely upon notes at all and they cite the example of Lord Birkenhead, who, I have been told, made no such notes. There are people with such a fantastic memory that they don't require these *aides-mémoire* but in my opinion the average person like me does require them very much indeed. Sometimes it may not be necessary to look at them at all, except at the very end of one's examination or cross-examination to see if one has left anything out. But the great point is that, if you have the notes on the table in front of you, you can concentrate entirely on the questions you are asking without worrying as to whether you may leave out something. The same applies to one's address to the judge or the jury. A comprehensive list of headings ensures that nothing will be omitted and that the fear that something may be left out will not be added to the strain which is upon every advocate when he presents his case.

Although the clerk in Le Quesne's chambers devoted himself immediately towards increasing my practice, with the result that it doubled itself in one year, my career at the Bar was advanced to a very large extent by the fact that I shared a room with Frank Gahan. He was a remarkable man, shy and self-effacing and therefore rather difficult to get to know. He was also a brilliant lawyer and, although not really suited to a High Court judgeship, because his work seldom involved examination and cross-examination of witnesses, he would have made a valuable addition to the Court of Appeal or even to the House of Lords. Most of his work when I came into chambers was in the Privy Council. In those days there were plenty of appeals from Canada, Australia and other places within the Commonwealth. In course of time Frank established such a reputation that, certainly in Canadian cases, he was usually on one side or the other. It was from him that I first learned to understand and apply the law, and any success which I may subsequently have attained is in great measure due to him. He became one of my greatest friends and it was a very sad blow to me when he died some two years ago.

It was after I had known him for about a couple of years that I did one of the stupidest things (unconnected with the law) which I have ever done. Frank's first wife was a neurotic and committed suicide. The same evening someone rang me up at home and told me about this and naturally I went straight down to see him. He asked me if I would go and break the news to his sister-in-law, who was in London. She was the widow of his late brother and she had a young family in Gloucestershire. I had never met her. I went straight off to the hotel in South Kensington where she was staying. I asked the manager whether I could see her and then I said to him (and this is something I have always regretted), 'Would you warn her, please, that she doesn't know me but I have very bad news for her.' I ought to have realized that this message, given to a mother of young children, would be bound to make her think that something had happened to one or other of them. The wretched woman came rushing to see me almost distraught. Although she was deeply distressed at the news which I gave her, she was at the same time immensely relieved, though she did not say so. Some people may think that I am too sensitive about the matter but, although the mother of the children is now dead, I still deeply regret having inflicted such terror upon her even for half a minute by my thoughtlessness.

I enjoyed myself in Le Quesne's chambers and eventually Frank and I virtually took them over when the increase in our practices justified our acquiring additional accommodation in the shape of the chambers below us.

Le Quesne never became a judge, though he went out as Commissioner of Assize on at least one occasion, obviously with a view to the Lord Chancellor considering whether he should be appointed. Unfortunately he was a worrier and, in the same way as he annoyed his clients by insisting on innumerable consultations, so he annoyed the Bar by the length of time which he took to try his cases. He was too meticulous. This was a pity because he was courteous, compassionate and, as I have said, a brilliant lawyer and those three qualities by themselves go a long way to the making of a first-class judge.

I only appeared very occasionally indeed in the Privy Council, but in one case, an appeal in a murder case from Malta, both sides wanted to brief Frank Gahan, so I was given the opportunity of appearing for the appellant. He was a policeman against whom the allegation was made that he arranged with a man to go away with his wife and murder her. Payment was to be by results. The man duly took the wife away but, having decided that she was rather a nice girl, he contented himself with sleeping with her and returned her to her husband the next morning in the same good condition in which he had received her.

According to the evidence of the prosecution, the policeman was not pleased but remained intent on carrying out his original plan. It was said that he then arranged with his brother and another man to take his wife away and throw her over a cliff. This time he was more successful. The unsuspecting lady went for a walk with the brother and the other man and, when they came to the top of the cliff, one of them pointed out to her some object on the horizon and said, 'Look', and, while she was looking, the other man pushed her over the cliff. Her body was discovered some days later. All the men in the case, except the

policeman, confessed to what they had done, but the policeman
denied having been party to any attempt to kill his wife. The
policeman and the two murderers were eventually all tried
together before the Chief Justice of Malta and a jury. The
policeman was found guilty and sentenced to death and he
appealed to the Privy Council. I appeared for him and Frank
appeared for the prosecution.

During the course of the hearing Lord Uthwatt, a very fine
lawyer, who unfortunately died when he had only been a short
time in the House of Lords, sent me this note:

Do you remember your Kai Lung stories? 'There are few problems
in life which cannot be solved by suicide, a bag of gold or by
thrusting a despised adversary over a cliff during the hours of
darkness.'

The main evidence against the policeman was, first, that of
the man who had slept with his wife and returned her in good
order and, secondly, the evidence of the fellow conspirators
who, having pleaded guilty to the charge, were called to give
evidence by the prosecution. There was a little evidence beside
this, but not very much. The only evidence in favour of the
policeman was his own. He went into the witness-box and
denied everything which was alleged against him. If the Chief
Justice had summed up properly to the jury and they had convicted my client, no appeal would have had any chance of
success. Someone may have written, or may some day write, the
story of a corrupt judge who wants to see a guilty man acquitted
and who therefore makes deliberate mistakes in his summing-up
so that an appeal against a verdict of guilty would be almost
certain to succeed. Such a situation is virtually impossible in
Britain where there has been no case of corruption against a
judge for well over 300 years. Nor do I think that there was the
slightest possibility that the Chief Justice of Malta was corrupt.
Had he been so, he would have found some more subtle way
to achieve his aim than by summing up as he did. For in his
summing up, having recited the evidence for the prosecution

at length and in detail, he then said to the jury, 'That, members of the jury, is the whole of the evidence.' He entirely omitted to tell them that my client had gone into the witness-box and sworn that the evidence for the prosecution was untrue. That the jury might have disbelieved such evidence is one thing, but the judge was bound to give them the opportunity of considering it.

In the result, on that ground alone the appeal was certain to succeed. But it was not surprising that a judge who could make such an incredible mistake in his summing-up made a good number of others, and I have never conducted an appeal which was so sure of success. Even Frank Gahan found it difficult to say anything in support of the conviction.

I did a certain amount of libel work and one of the most interesting cases in which I was engaged was interesting not so much for the subject-matter as for the clash between two members of the Bar. They were both K.C.s and they both subsequently became High Court judges. I have said before that the Bar is an extremely friendly profession but naturally you do occasionally get barristers who dislike each other and that was the case on this occasion. A man called Hayley Morris had been convicted of various sexual offences with young girls. This was a time when, once a man was convicted, the Press were rather inclined to say all sorts of things which they couldn't possibly prove about him. When Hayley Morris came out of prison from serving his sentence of three years he proceeded to take action against many of the newspapers which had libelled him. He also sued the author and publishers of a book in which it was in effect alleged that he had been guilty of rape. Now this was untrue, as in all cases where he had committed a sexual offence the girls concerned had consented. Gerald Slade was appearing for the publishers and I was appearing for the author. Hayley Morris had been defended by Roland Oliver when he was prosecuted and he called him to give evidence on his behalf. Roland Oliver was blind in one eye and wore an eye-glass, and he had, I should think, the smoothest manner of anyone at the Bar. Slade proceeded to cross-examine him about Hayley Morris and to indulge in one of the silly exaggerations in which I am afraid some lawyers, and even some judges, do occasionally indulge.

'Can you think,' he asked Roland Oliver, 'of a worse case than Hayley Morris's?'

Roland Oliver adjusted his eye-glass and said: 'I beg your pardon?'

Slade was compelled to repeat his question. 'Can I think of a worse case?' repeated Oliver. 'Of course I can. Many worse. Murder, rape, blackmail. Hayley Morris's was a bad case, because he often imposed upon the mothers of these young girls, but all the young girls were consenting parties. But a worse case! I can't think you mean it.'

Slade was a good lawyer and an able advocate. When he became a judge, people worried lest he would remain an advocate on the Bench because at the Bar he threw himself wholeheartedly into the fight and fought for his client almost as hard as Marshall Hall. I say 'almost' because Marshall Hall did not always keep his advocacy within proper bounds. Slade in fact turned out to be an unsatisfactory judge but not for the reason that had been anticipated by the people who doubted the wisdom of his appointment. So far from being an advocate on the Bench, he had great difficulty in making up his mind and he took a very long time about it.

Oliver was a much better judge, because normally he was quite capable of making up his mind, although he was only a moderate lawyer. There was a case, however, in which Oliver had difficulty in making up his mind and I must say I sympathized with him. He simply could not decide in a certain accident case whether the plaintiff was over the white line in the middle of the road or whether the defendant was. He found that all the witnesses were honest but he simply could not decide between them. He therefore held that the plaintiff had failed in his claim and that the defendant had failed in his counter-claim because neither of them had proved his case. Both parties appealed to the Court of Appeal, who said that it was a judge's duty to make up his mind, and they sent the case back for a new trial. I should have thought it was also a judge's duty not to *pretend* to have made up his mind when he had not in fact done so. The Court of Appeal would not have criticized Oliver if (without admitting it) he had tossed up for the result in his own mind but had stated in court that he accepted the evidence given on behalf of the plaintiff or the defendant, as the case might be.

Roland Oliver led me in a case of criminal conspiracy in which a number of men were charged with conspiracy to sell as a well-known brand of contraceptive pieces of soap made to look like the genuine article. They forged literature to look exactly like the genuine literature which was inserted by the manufacturers in the boxes containing the contraceptives. They also forged the labels outside those boxes. In addition, they made cartons to resemble the manufacturers' cartons. At cut prices they sold to chemists large numbers of these cartons which contained boxes for retail sale to the public. The manufacturers naturally became extremely worried when they found these fraudulent pieces of soap being sold under their name.

The lack of any contraceptive quality whatever in the pieces of soap must have led to the birth of a good number of unwanted children. But, although it might have been possible to prove that the conspirators were directly responsible for some of these births, they could not have been adjudged to have been the putative fathers of those children. Nevertheless, a claim for damages could have been made against them by involuntary parents. But the amount of the damages would have been difficult to ascertain and, as criminals rarely have any traceable funds with which to pay such damages, no one ever thought of suing them.

The manufacturers were determined, if possible, to bring the conspirators to account in the criminal courts, and so they employed an excellent middle-aged detective, who was as unlike Sherlock Holmes or any detective in fiction as it was possible to imagine. He was extremely efficient and managed to trace one of the conspirators and obtain his confidence. The conspirator told the detective that they were having some diffi-

culty in making cartons to resemble exactly the cartons which
the genuine manufacturers supplied. The detective told the
man that he thought he might be able to help him. He then
arranged with the manufacturers to supply him with genuine
cartons which were secretly marked. After they had been
supplied for a little time, one of the conspirators complained
that some of the cartons were not sufficiently like the genuine
ones and told the detective that he must take more care in his
next deliveries. When we considered that we had sufficient
evidence the police were informed and they duly arrested all the
conspirators but one. He was caught about a year later. All the
men concerned were sentenced to imprisonment, the judge
saying that it was a cruel and heartless fraud.

*

At a time when I had given up going to County Courts and
magistrates' courts, I was asked by a client of mine whether I
would make an exception and appear for a man at Marl-
borough Street Magistrates' Court. He was charged with
importuning for immoral purposes in a public lavatory. When
my clerk came to me and asked if I would do the case he told
me that he had said to the client that it wasn't the sort of work
I did, but that the solicitor had pleaded with him, saying that
it was not an ordinary case at all, that the accused was a very
decent chap, that he was a B.B.C. singer, and that he would be
ruined if he were sent to prison and that there really were
special circumstances. Would I, at any rate, see him and the
client? I said I would.

It was an almost invariable practice then for magistrates to
send to prison anyone convicted of that offence and the magistrate
before whom the man was going to appear was Mr Sandbach.
He was a very nice down-to-earth magistrate, but he was pretty
old-fashioned in his ideas. Homosexuals were anathema to him.

I saw the man and it was certainly a rather tragic case. The
facts which I am about to mention were stated in court so that
there is no reason why I should not mention them. The
accused was a homosexual from birth and in his twenties he had

tried hard to overcome his natural inclinations. Eventually he succeeded and married. It was a very happy marriage, but after two or three years the wife died in childbirth. The husband was grief-stricken and eventually returned to his old practices. It was not long after this that he was charged with the particular offence. But fortunately he had two great friends, a doctor and his wife, who were prepared to do everything they could to help him and in particular to come to court and say that they would be happy for him to come and live with them for an indefinite period. It seemed to me that on these facts it would be very wrong indeed to send this man to prison and I said I would take the case. I warned my client, however, that it would be a very difficult task to avoid imprisonment before Sandbach.

However, as an advocate anxious to succeed on behalf of my client, I had a very pleasant surprise when I reached the court. The solicitor introduced me to the doctor and his wife, and the wife was one of the most beautiful girls I had seen. When the accused met them in the lobby of the court the girl kissed him with great affection. I have said that Mr Sandbach was old-fashioned and I was morally certain that he would be quite old-fashioned enough to be very much attracted to this young woman.

Often in these cases the charge used to be disputed because a conviction would mean imprisonment. When the case was called on, I said that I appeared for the accused and that he was going to plead guilty. After the charge had been read out and the solicitor for the prosecution had stated the facts, Mr Sandbach turned to me and asked me without much enthusiasm if there was anything I wanted to say in mitigation. I said that there was indeed and that I ventured to think that it was different from any other case which the magistrate had tried. Mr Sandbach was quite a sentimental man and I felt sure that the story of my client would have some effect on him. Having, as it were, slightly conditioned the magistrate by reciting the distressing facts of the wife's death, I then said that I was going to call the doctor and his wife who were prepared to look after my client if the magistrate would put him on probation. I said that I was going to call the wife first. Then I called this beautiful girl into the witness-box. It was a very effective moment. I won't say that the magistrate was visibly affected, but I felt sure that he had never seen a girl of this kind called to give evidence in a case where a man was charged with importuning men in a public lavatory. The fact that she was on the side of the accused seemed to be a contradiction in terms. She gave her evidence extremely well, with controlled emotion and in a clear voice which the magistrate had no difficulty in hearing. When she had finished I knew that we had won. But, having decided that he was going to take a lenient course, Mr Sandbach could not resist giving rein to his hatred of homosexuals.

'In all the circumstances,' he said, 'I am going to bind you over for two years. I find it hard to believe that you have such wonderful friends. Or, indeed, that you can find anyone to shake you by the hand. But, having heard the evidence, for the very special reasons which exist in this case I am not going to send you to prison.'

The members of the Press were also obviously affected by the circumstances because, knowing that to mention the man's name would do him considerable harm, they didn't mention the case at all. Outside court the lovely girl embraced my client again. A little enviously I left the court.

*

One of my greatest triumphs arose out of a case which had to do with electricity. I'm extremely bad at dealing with technical matters of this kind. I knew nothing whatever about electricity. I knew that, if you turned on a switch and there was nothing wrong, a light would come on, but I didn't really know why. So, in order to understand the case, I had to start from the very beginning and to read elementary books and consult experts on the subject. I did a tremendous amount of work and, when I went into court, I felt satisfied that I really did know sufficient about electricity to understand everything about the case. Such confidence, if not misplaced, is important. I duly fought the case and lost it. But I came home and I mended a lamp. I was right in thinking that I had learned something about electricity.

I cannot say why, but cases about drains and sewers rather interested me. I once had a case before the Tottenham justices where my clients were charged with some offence connected with drains. They were convicted. They had been prosecuted by the local council and at least two of the three justices who had convicted my client had at one time been members of that council. It may be that all three had been. The decision was quite wrong in law and I advised my clients to appeal to the High Court. This they did and the appeal was duly allowed and the conviction quashed. However, the High Court had no power to order the payment to my clients of the original costs of the hearing before the justices at Tottenham. So later on I applied to the justices for the payment of those costs. The matter was argued at some length by me and my opponent and then the justices conferred without leaving the court. I heard one of them say, 'We've lost and I think we ought to pay.' And they duly ordered the council to pay the costs.

The system of Justices of the Peace works very well and, although decisions of various Benches can be criticized, just as decisions of judges can be criticized, on the whole they do their work extremely well and they are quite irreplaceable. But, as on the occasion to which I have referred, it must sometimes be difficult for them to hear dispassionately claims by or against local authorities of which they may have been members for some years.

*

Lawyers do not like coincidences when the guilt or innocence of their client depends upon one. But undoubtedly very odd coincidences do occur. For example, I once had a case which lasted several days at the Old Bailey. It was one in which my clients, who were bookmakers, were charged with bribing or attempting to bribe the police. After a hearing lasting several days they were both acquitted. It was a very strange case. During it I called a police officer to give evidence on behalf of my clients. This witness swore that a detective-sergeant, who had given evidence against my clients, had said in the police

D

canteen that my clients had given him more money than he had put in the charge, in other words that he had kept part of the money for himself. My witness also swore that the same sergeant and another police officer had from time to time in the past persuaded him to commit perjury in the magistrates' court in other cases. Such evidence meant that the witness whom I had called must have committed perjury at some stage. Either he was committing perjury in his evidence at the Old Bailey or he had committed perjury in other cases in other courts. In consequence, he was suspended from duty and there was a police enquiry into the whole matter. What happened at that enquiry I do not know, but I do know that he was restored to his position with full pay from the beginning of his suspension.

Not long before this case, I was sitting in a train when a man approached me and asked me if I had not been counsel in some case or other in a magistrates' court. I said that I had been and it turned out that he was one of the J.P.s who had decided the case. Because of this experience I tried to memorize the face of the foreman of the jury in the bribery case so that, if I happened to meet him later, I could ask him questions about the case, which would not involve the disclosure of any secrets of the jury room.

Nothing happened for some time, but it was just about then that my wife and I had become very fond of music and, as we were gramophone-taught, we started to buy records in very large quantities. We used to go to His Master's Voice shop in Oxford Street and we were always looked after by the same assistant.

We got to know the girl quite well and she became a friend of ours. One day she said: 'D'you know, my father heard you at the Old Bailey some time ago.' He turned out to be the foreman of the jury in the bribery case.

*

One of the problems which faces a newly-called barrister is to decide to what extent he should rely on and follow the instructions which he has been given. In *Brothers in Law* I gave an example of this kind of thing. Roger Thursby was cross-examining a witness when he was suddenly told by a managing clerk of his instructing solicitors to ask the witness whether he had ever been bankrupt. This is the kind of thing which sometimes happens to a barrister. When he is an experienced practitioner he knows what to do about it. But when he is very little experienced or wholly inexperienced it is a very serious problem. When he receives the instructions in chambers he can take advice from older men there. But when he is suddenly told to ask the question in court he often simply does not know what to do. If he doesn't ask the question, his clients may not be pleased and, if he loses the case, they may never come to him again. If he does ask the question and it turns out to be a foolish one, he may lose the case in consequence. In *Brothers in Law* Roger Thursby did ask the question and, in consequence, got into the most hopeless difficulties. The situation was in no way exaggerated. I only learned about these matters by experiencing them. This is the best way to learn, but it is also the most painful. And when I had pupils of my own I certainly tried to give them advice which might have the effect of their avoiding a number of the disasters which I experienced.

In this connection I remember once receiving instructions from solicitors who cannot have been of the highest class. The instructions told me that the plaintiff, for whom I was appearing, was extremely ill but at the end of them was a P.S. as follows: 'The plaintiff is now dead but counsel will no doubt do his best to cover this.'

Fortunately at the time I received these instructions I was sufficiently experienced to appreciate their impropriety, but it could have given me an idea for Roger Thursby. He could have been on his feet in the County Court and have just said: 'I'll call the plaintiff, your Honour,' when the solicitor whispers to him: 'You can't. He's dead, but don't tell the judge.'

'Well, Mr Thursby,' the judge would say, 'are we going to have the pleasure of seeing your client in the witness-box? I've been waiting half a minute since you said you were going to call him.'

'Your Honour,' begins Roger, but, as on previous occasions, he does not know how to follow it up.

'You were about to say?' asks the judge.

'Your Honour –' says Roger.

'I follow that,' says the judge, 'but what comes after?'

Unfortunately I never thought of inserting such a scene and so I shall never know what came after.

*

Although my own ability is strictly limited, I hope that I am not too immodest in saying that I am quite good at recognizing high ability in others.

I remember hearing a young junior arguing a case. I did not know who he was but I was very much struck by his ability. Indeed, I really wondered whether there was any point in my continuing at the Bar when some unknown young man was so much my superior. He was to become Lord Devlin.

Again, I remember a case in which I was opposed by Lord Denning when he was a junior. We eventually settled the case and we had a fair number of interviews in the course of our negotiations. I soon realized what a fine lawyer he was and again I wondered what I was doing at the Bar when there were juniors whose knowledge and grasp of the law were so infinitely above mine.

I must say that I was extremely pleased when both these young men went to the top of the profession.

As my practice gradually increased I began to require assistance myself and I was very lucky in at least two of the 'devils' who assisted me. One was Quintin Hogg, who subsequently became Lord Chancellor, and the other Brian Mackenna, who subsequently became Mr Justice Mackenna. I have little doubt that, when they did work for me, the 'devilling' system proved an advantage to my clients.

At one time I used to devil for Sir Leslie Scott, who subsequently became Lord Justice Scott. He paid me nothing, which was just about what I was worth to him, but the experience was valuable to me. I remember on one occasion that he had a difficult case involving both United States and English law. It was about machinery for making shoes. I attended a consultation at which Sir Leslie Scott presided. The other members of the Bar were Lord Macmillan, who was then a silk, and J. H. Stamp, who was one of the ablest juniors at the Chancery Bar. When the problems were discussed, the only good thing which Sir Leslie Scott did was to say nothing. Apparently he too could recognize in Macmillan and Stamp minds which were far superior to his.

*

Probably the reason why some criminals specialize is because it is so much easier to deal in one commodity only. You know where it can be obtained, how to dispose of it, what the risks are in obtaining it and so forth. For somewhat similar reasons it is possible to specialize at the Bar. And specialist counsel, however successful he may be, normally has a much easier time than the general practitioner. Although difficult questions of law can arise in any case, it is a tremendous advantage to a practising lawyer to know the law thoroughly on any particular subject. He knows if the law is quite certain and he knows where there are gaps. And, better still, he knows exactly where to look for them. To make a sufficient income he must specialize in a subject about which there is sufficient litigation or at any rate enough advice sought.

The most profitable of all subjects is revenue law. But it is very difficult to get into revenue chambers. Revenue counsel do not normally take pupils and, although this practice may be a little more relaxed now, it is almost impossible to get into revenue chambers unless you have special credentials, e.g. unless you were a tax inspector or in the Board of Inland Revenue before you were called to the Bar. But once there, a very sound financial future is assured. Revenue work is highly paid. A profitable part of it consists in preparing statements by taxpayers who have defrauded the Revenue and who are prepared to pay a very large sum to avoid prosecution. The Revenue has the right in such cases, if it thinks fit and there is full disclosure by the taxpayer, to accept a sum sufficient to satisfy its claims instead of initiating prosecution.

I once did a patent action at the request of a client of mine who had more confidence in me than he had common sense. It was very foolish of me to do this, because, although I hope I was capable of looking up the law and the practice on the subject, there are many things that happen in the courts which are not strictly laid down in any book. You can only know them by experience. In consequence, I expect I made a pretty good mess of the case. I never did a patent case again.

I did quite an amount of copyright work. Most solicitors and some counsel think that all copyright actions are tried in the Chancery Division. But there is no rule to this effect and when I advised my clients to take proceedings, I always advised them to take them in the King's Bench Division. I did this for two reasons. First, because the defendant's solicitors would probably instruct Chancery counsel. Just as King's Bench counsel sometimes feel uncomfortable in a Chancery Court, so Chancery counsel sometimes feel uncomfortable in a King's Bench Court. Secondly, it was probable that, as I did a good deal of this work, my knowledge of copyright law would be greater than a King's Bench judge's.

One of the most interesting copyright cases which I had was brought on behalf of the sister of the late H. H. Munro (Saki) who was killed in the first war. His sister was his administratrix.

The decision in this case involved two points of law which had never previously been decided and fortunately we had a very good judge, the then Mr Justice Du Parcq, to decide them. Saki had written a story called *The Interlopers* and a man (who disappeared when trouble started) proceeded to plagiarize the story and sell the result to the *Evening News*. The editor, who did not remember or was unaware of the Saki story, published the story in good faith. One of the defences raised by the proprietors of the *Evening News* was the defence of innocent publication. The section of the Copyright Act 1911 dealing with this matter was Section 8 and the side note to the section is 'Exemption of innocent infringers from liability to pay damages'. A layman could certainly be forgiven for thinking that, if he published copyright matter quite innocently, he would not be liable in damages to the owner of the copyright. When he gave evidence I asked the editor of the *Evening News* two questions:

'You believed that copyright existed in the story which the man sent you?'

'Yes.'

'You thought that the copyright belonged to him?'

'Yes.'

Mr Justice Du Parcq held that these two answers prevented the newspaper from relying upon the defence of innocent publication, as such a defence, on a true construction of the section, was only open to someone who did not believe that copyright existed in the work which he published.

The *Evening News* was therefore liable to pay damages to Miss Munro but how much? Under the then Copyright Act every copy of the offending work belonged to my client. The *Evening News* received one penny for each copy sold, less the costs of distribution. The judge accepted the argument, which has since been upheld in the House of Lords, that the measure of damages was so much of the amount received by the *Evening News* as would be equivalent to the proportion of space which the offending story bore to the whole newspaper. In evaluating the matter, not only the actual space taken up by the story had to be considered but the value of it to the public. Some people might buy the *Evening News* simply for the news. Others would buy it for the advertisements only. Others still for the story. The court would have to do the best it could to arrive at a fair decision.

Advocates

There is a danger to the legal profession in the sudden emergence of the Bar as a lucrative profession for almost anyone who gets into it. And the danger is that, if a person can acquire a substantial practice, whether (within certain limitations) he does his work well or badly, it is a grave temptation to the lazier man not to worry too much how he gets up his cases. When I was a judge I found that comparatively few young barristers came to court knowing sufficiently the law and practice which applied to their cases, and many of them were at the Common Law Bar, where the standard is higher than at the Criminal Bar. Avory, as I have said, was a good lawyer though not a great one, but his very high reputation as a criminal lawyer was partly due to the fact that so very few criminal practitioners were anything but moderate lawyers.

If the standard at the Bar is not to go down it is vital that pupil-masters and judges should do all they can to persuade young barristers to go meticulously into the law of every case with which they are concerned. Indeed, some strong doses of Hill Kelly would be of great value to the Bar.

Whether or not he is conceited by nature, it is very difficult for the young barrister not to become so. There are very few modest members of the Bar and I was certainly not one of them. Although the abolition of the death penalty has done away with some of the glamour of the Bar, people are still interested in the law, not least because they have a wholesome fear of it.

Accordingly I expect that young barristers are still asked in almost reverential terms questions like these:

'Are you a barrister? Have you done any murder cases?'

As a barrister has to assert himself in court and as in private he is often looked upon with at least a certain amount of awe and as he spends a proportion of his time acting a part, it would be difficult for the average young person not to begin to think too much of himself. It is true that there is no applause after he has made his speech or concluded his cross-examination, but he is speaking before an audience in public and to some extent is therefore in the same position as an actor. Most actors and actresses are charming people, they are generous and kind and make excellent friends, but few of them can be said to be modest. I should think that the Bar and the stage are about equal in this respect.

One of the ablest and most pleasant opponents I found myself against was Walter Monckton (later Viscount Monckton of Brenchley), who became Attorney-General to the Prince of Wales and was much concerned in the abdication of Edward VIII. He had been four years at the Bar when I was called, and I was against him on a number of occasions before and after he took silk in 1930. He also led me in a case just before I became a judge. Since his death a few people have said unkind things about Walter Monckton. I can only say that I never heard him say an unkind word about anyone and that, while at the Bar, his conduct towards his colleagues, towards witnesses and towards the Bench, was as good an example of the way a barrister should behave as I know.

Another of the ablest members of the Bar during the whole of my time at the Bar was Sir Valentine Holmes. He looked anything but a successful advocate. He had a pale face and a slightly bulbous reddish nose, and was the son of a distinguished Irish judge and was expected by the Bar to go on the English Bench. But any layman, being told this and seeing him appear in court, would have been extremely surprised. For not only had he a somewhat unattractive appearance, which was certainly no indication of his scholarship, brain-power or advocacy, but he had a hesitant manner. He must have realized at some stage in his career what a tremendous power he was in the courts and with what respect the judges listened to him. But his hesitancy continued. He was thirty-four when I came to the Bar and up to a period not long before this he had mainly devilled for Leslie Scott, in whose chambers he was. Eventually, however, he started to acquire a large practice of his own and in the end he must have been easily the busiest junior at the Common Law Bar. He was a very fine lawyer, had a very wide knowledge of practice and procedure, and was very popular with all his colleagues. He was always extremely kind and helpful to me. He became the Common Law Treasury junior and he took silk at the end of the second war.

Although no one would have chosen Valentine Holmes as a great advocate he was none the less an immediate success as a silk. This was because of his supreme ability and because, in spite of his hesitancy, he knew exactly how to put forward a case before a judge and it was almost a certainty that, if his clients were in the right, they would succeed.

Valentine Holmes became a great friend of his clerk and the two of them used to go regularly to watch greyhound racing and I believe that one or other or both of them owned a greyhound. It is stated in the *Dictionary of National Biography* that he was offered a High Court judgeship and that he refused. I was unaware of this and had thought it possible that the then Lord Chancellor was disinclined to offer a judgeship to someone who went regularly to the dogs. Holmes's failure to become a judge was in all probability a very great loss to the Bench. He would have brought to it not only his great knowledge of law and his ability to apply it to the facts of a case but courtesy and care, and he would probably have been one of the outstanding judges of the twentieth century. He would have been very likely indeed to have become a law lord. However, eventually he retired from the Bar and went as legal adviser to a very large industrial company.

Other first-rate lawyers when I came to the Bar were S. L. Porter (later Lord Porter), who was still a junior, A. T. Miller,

F. Q. M. Schiller and Stuart Bevan. Both Miller and Schiller must have refused High Court judgeships, because they were at the top of their profession and excellent lawyers. Miller would certainly have been likely to have made a first-class judge. It was said that Stuart Bevan either refused or was never offered a judgeship for domestic reasons. He was a very fine lawyer and advocate and had a charming personality.

Famous advocates of my early days were Simon, Jowitt, Hogg, Marshall Hall, Patrick Hastings and, a little later, Norman Birkett. I think that I only heard Marshall Hall once. This was in the divorce court when he was appearing for a man who was said to have committed adultery with a woman then dead, and who was resisting a claim for damages from the husband. Marshall Hall did not speak for long but he devoted a fair part of his speech to an attack upon his opponent. In effect he said to the jury that he couldn't believe that a member of an honourable profession like the Bar could consent to appear for a man who was publicizing his wife's shame after her death in order to make money. It was a very effective attack but grossly unfair. His opponent was a member of the Divorce Bar, and, as Marshall Hall well knew, was bound to accept the brief, however distasteful the subject-matter might be. I was led by A. T. Miller, Stuart Bevan, Patrick Hastings and Norman Birkett but, except in the lamentable instance of my appearing as a pupil when Simon was leading Fortune, never by any of the others.

One of Patrick Hastings' successes in the Criminal Courts was that of Mrs Barney, who was charged with murder. I had a watching brief for someone who was concerned in the case. Mrs Barney was a woman who was alleged to have shot her lover and evidence was given of shots being fired on previous occasions from the mews house where she lived. Evidence about these additional shots was given by one or two witnesses and I was surprised to find that Patrick Hastings asked none of the questions which I would have asked had I been in his position. I discovered the reason when he made his final speech. The police had never been called on any of these occasions and I would have asked the witnesses why, if they were sure that what they had heard had been shots, they didn't go and call the police. Patrick Hastings asked them nothing on the subject, but in his final speech he said most effectively to the jury:

'Are there no police in Paddington? Is it conceivable, members of the jury, that if these witnesses really heard what they believed to be shots from a firearm they would not have gone running out to find the nearest policeman? If it really happened, why not?'

It must be remembered that Patrick Hastings was defending and a good deal of licence is allowed to advocates defending prisoners charged with murder. Strictly speaking, I suppose, it can be said that he ought to have given the opportunity to those witnesses whose evidence he was going to criticize to explain why they had not gone for a policeman. But had he done so, they might have given some good, bad or indifferent explanation which might have taken the edge off the point which he made so effectively in his final speech to the jury. It was certainly a lesson in economy in cross-examination.

Later on, when I was a judge, I tried a case where experienced and able counsel must have deeply regretted after the case that he hadn't practised economy in *his* cross-examination. It was a road accident case and the plaintiff's evidence was that he was driving his car up a hill when the defendant appeared at the top of the hill where there was a bend. He said that the defendant's car came too fast to take the bend, swerved across the road and hit him head on. In support of his case the plaintiff called a witness who said that he was wheeling his bicycle up the hill when he saw the accident take place. He confirmed what the plaintiff had said. He was then cross-examined by the defendant's counsel.

'You say that my client came round the top of the hill very fast?'

'Yes.'

'How fast would you say?'

'About sixty or thereabouts.'

Are you a good judge of speed?'

'Yes.'

'D'you drive a car or a motor-cycle?'

'No.'

That was the time to stop, but counsel went on:

'What do you do?' he asked.

'I'm an engine-driver,' was the reply.

It is true to say that, had counsel not asked that question, I should probably have asked it myself, but nevertheless it was a very good example of one question too many being asked.

❈ The Adjutant Who Knew Too Much

After I had been in Le Quesne's chambers for a short time I was earning just enough to do something which in some ways gave me a good deal more pleasure than anything I had done up to then. My parents, as I have said, were not well off; it was not remotely possible for them to have a car and they had never even considered it. In 1930 my brother Walter and I gave them a car and a chauffeur. (To begin with it was a chauffeuse.) Without telling them anything about it at all, we were able one day to ask them to come downstairs as we had a little surprise for them. My father must have had a suspicion that something exciting was in the offing because I still remember the look on his face of pleasure and anticipation and some excitement as he ran down the stairs leading to the front door. My mother followed more sedately. Outside was an Armstrong Siddeley saloon car with a sliding roof, which had been manufactured the year before. My father lived for another four years after this and the pleasure which this car gave to him and my mother during that period was even beyond our expectations. The chauffeuse was shortly afterwards replaced by a chauffeur who was able to take complete charge of the car.

We had bought the car second-hand from a dealer who had assured us that it was in perfect working order. Within a week smoke was pouring into the car from the engine and a rebore became immediately necessary. I had not been prepared to accept the assurances of the dealer from whom I bought the car, because, after all, I was now a barrister of some six years' experience and had learned (so I thought) a certain amount about the ways of car dealers. I also decided that I knew better than the A.A. and the R.A.C., and would employ a motor engineer who regularly gave evidence in accident cases. I later explained to my parents, perhaps rather complacently, that as a result of my experience at the Bar I knew just the sort of engineer to employ. So the engineer of my choice examined the car and told me that it was in good working order and that I could safely accept it. I proceeded to question him about the car and suppose I must have tried on him some of my gradually increasing powers of cross-examination. Eventually he asked me if I thought he was being paid anything by the dealer. Until he said this I hadn't the slightest suspicion that this might have happened, but when a week later I had to pay for a rebore, I just wondered.

Frank Gahan married again very happily in 1934 and in 1935 I married Lettice Apperly with whom I was intensely happy until her death in 1950. By the time I married, I was earning enough to live such a life in comfort. My father had died in 1934. Lettice and I occupied the upper part of my mother's house in Bayswater, while my mother and Walter, who was as yet unmarried, occupied the lower half. I sometimes find it difficult now to believe that before the war I was able to afford to have a cook and maid living in, a charwoman and a woman to do the sewing who came in regularly, and a chauffeur. And I paid them what were then considered good wages.

Although I had to work very hard, we had a wonderful time until the war came. And even the war brought us some good fortune because in 1942 my battalion was stationed in a little village in Kent called Milstead. As adjutant I was given the job of going to see the rector to ask him if we could put a Bren gun on the top of the church at Milstead. The rector, the Reverend Edward Taylor-Jones, in spite of a permanent limp, had been a fine cricketer in his day. He was a great patriot and a splendid parson. He lived in Kingsdown Rectory where there was another church. This was a couple of miles from Milstead. He had no doubt whatever that God was on our side and he was therefore delighted to give permission for the Bren gun to be put into position. But his Bishop had other views and thought that churches should not be used as implements of war. So it had to be taken down again.

But, when I went to see the rector, I achieved something more important from my point of view than permission to put up the Bren gun. Mrs Taylor-Jones asked me if any officers in our battalion had wives who would care sometimes to come and spend the week-end there. I immediately asked if I might use the telephone. I rang Lettice, she came down the next day and stayed with them for the rest of the war. The Taylor-Joneses have been friends of ours ever since. In spite of the fact that the rectory had no water, electricity or gas laid on and that in consequence the bath had to be filled from water obtained from a nearby well, Lettice loved it there. She is now buried within fifty yards of the house in Kingsdown churchyard.

Lettice came from a Gloucestershire family who had lived in Stroud for many years. Her mother was a very keen amateur cellist and for a long time, even after she became quite old, she was Secretary of the Strolling Players' Amateur Orchestra. Her father was the most skilful dentist for whom I have ever opened my mouth.

*

The prospects of another war seemed considerable in 1938, and, as Walter and I had both missed the First World War, we thought that, if there were a second, we couldn't decently miss that. So, after Munich, we joined the Army Officers' Emergency Reserve, an excellent organization which ensured that you only joined the Army if a war actually took place.

In due course Walter went into the East Surreys and I went into the Queen's (West Surreys). I can't pretend that I liked the idea of the Army. I don't much care for giving orders and still less like receiving them. But a few years in the Army was likely to make up to some extent for the fact that I had started at the Bar too young. Like other young people at the beginning of a career I wanted to begin as soon as possible, but in fact a young man of twenty-five or twenty-six or even older is much better equipped for a career at the Bar than a boy or girl of twenty-one, who only has experience of school and university and perhaps of washing up in restaurants during the vacations. I did not even have that last advantage and really had wholly insufficient knowledge of life to justify me in conducting cases which were of importance to the people for whom I was appearing.

I was commissioned off the streets and, although I had been in the O.T.C. at school, I had long ago forgotten any military knowledge which I might have had. Shortly after being commissioned I was sent to an officers' training unit, where I was taught how to 'make an appreciation'. It is one of the few things which I learned in the Army and which I have always remembered. An appreciation is simply the consideration of all those matters which you have to bear in mind before you embark on a certain course of action. Sometimes in ordinary life you make many appreciations in the course of a day. When you want to decide what play to go to see, where to go for a holiday, whether to apply for a particular job, whether to dismiss an employee or the like, consciously or unconsciously you weigh up the pros and cons of the situation before you make your decision.

The mystic initials which we were taught were O.C.C.P., which I have never forgotten, because the mnemonic for the first three letters is OLD CHELTONIANS CANNOT. I shall never know why Cheltonians were chosen. O stands for object. The first C stands for considerations affecting the attainment of the object, the second C stands for 'courses open'. This is subdivided into (a) courses open to you and (b) courses open to the enemy. (In ordinary life the enemy may be, for example, time or your mother-in-law or the weather.) Finally P stands for plan.

The important one to remember is O. Before you make a
plan in war you have to decide, for example, whether your
object is to capture the hill or to kill the enemy who holds it.
Your plan may be very different according to your object. The
same applies to ordinary life. If you have received a letter which
has annoyed you and you are about to reply, what object do
you want to achieve by your reply? If you want to satisfy your
sense of indignation, you write one sort of letter. If you want to
maintain a pleasant relationship between you and your correspondent, you would write another sort of letter. Over the
years I have altered my provisional decisions in my private life
on a fair number of occasions by forcing myself to consider what
my real object is.

I cannot pretend that I distinguished myself as a military
lawyer. To have a real knowledge of military law you have to
read the Army Act and King's Regulations and in wartime
there are many more things for an officer in an ordinary infantry
battalion to do than to study those matters. But I brought with
me the confidence of sixteen years' practice at the Bar and,
while this was an advantage in some respects, confidence without a firm basis for it (i.e. without a good knowledge of the
Army Act and King's Regulations) can be disastrous. But if you
are in the Army in wartime, and have had anything to do with
the law in civilian life, you are liable to be pressed into service
by anyone from the C.O. to the sanitary man. I am referring
to those who have been on the right side of the law. But in fact
use can be made of those who have been on the other side of the
law. Burglars, for example, can be very helpful in an emergency and, indeed, acting on a well-known principle, I once
recommended that a burglar be made a provost-lance-corporal.
The strain of having to distinguish between his own and other
people's property, however, proved too much for him.

But, if you've been respectably in law, it's assumed by everyone that no legal problem is too difficult for you. If anyone is
to be court-martialled, you will be detailed to defend him,
poor fellow. If some knotty legal question arises, your advice
will be sought. Protestations that the particular aspect of the

law concerned is not in your line will not help you in the least. You've been in the law, you know it all.

In my case not only had I been engaged in the law before I went into the Army but what is more I thought I knew something about it. I made no modest protests and I willingly placed my knowledge and experience at the disposal of anyone who chose to ask for my help.

*

I started life in my battalion as a platoon commander. Fortunately I was quite fit, because I had been accustomed to run round Hyde Park six days a week to keep in reasonable condition. I didn't go very fast and, although I sometimes resented having to get up so early in the morning, once I was out in the Park I liked it. And it was interesting to see some of the people who were there at that time. I remember once being amused by a man, who was doing the same as I was, being chased by about a dozen dogs which a lady had taken out for exercise. I was not so much amused a few days later when they chased me, and I referred the lady to the Park regulations. Having been fit was an advantage to me when I had to lead the life of a platoon commander at the age of thirty-eight, but fitness was not always enough. On one occasion we were doing some platoon exercise and we came to the top of a wall from which there was quite a big drop down. I was on top of the wall with the sergeant and some of the men. They seemed a little hesitant to jump, so I prepared to do so.

'I shouldn't at your age,' whispered the sergeant.

There was no help for it then. I had to jump. I did, and sprained an ankle and having to pretend that I hadn't was one of my most unpleasant experiences during the war. Possibly as a result of this exploit I was made assistant adjutant and had to go to the orderly room and leave the platoon for ever. I am glad to say that my batman, Henry Thompson, came with me and he was with me for my whole period with the battalion. At the end of the Tunisian campaign he caused me to be knocked unconscious by an iron bar. But we are still the best of friends.

He had an extraordinary war. He was in it from the start, was at Dunkirk, went through the whole of the North African campaign, went to Italy and finally to Europe and was completely unscathed until the day before the Armistice, when he shot himself through the foot with a revolver. If he had done that at an earlier stage in the war, people might have suspected that it was an intentionally self-inflicted wound. I would have been sure that it wasn't, but, as it is a well-recognized method of avoiding the even less pleasant consequences of battle, he might have been in some difficulty. But nobody could have believed that anyone would have done such a thing on the day before the Armistice. Apart from that fact, I could well believe that he could have done anything with a revolver. He had never learned to use one and, even if he had, I don't suppose he would have been much better at it than I was. People who have not used revolvers do not realize how difficult it is to aim straight or to hit even quite a large target. Although it is possible that a lady with a small revolver might hit a man at the other end of a room, the chances are that she would miss him altogether. Thomp (as I used to call him, pronouncing the Th as in thing) may have been aiming at a target twenty yards away, or, more probably, thought it was unloaded.

When I heard of his exploit I remember that, when he was in my platoon and I was inspecting the guard of which he was a member, he was told to ease springs and, on doing so, produced five live rounds out of his rifle. The sergeant and I were so surprised that no proceedings were taken against him. In any event, I hadn't the faintest idea what to do about it. This was when we were stationed at Long Sutton, expecting the German invasion. So perhaps Thomp wanted to make sure that at least one person had a round up the spout.

A court of enquiry was convened to consider the shooting accident and it completely cleared him.

*

One of the first cases I came across in the orderly room was a file labelled *The Elusive Private Amass*. He had gone absent without leave, had been arrested and brought back to the battalion, had escaped and was again arrested and brought back. I was given the job of prosecuting him for desertion.

In order to prove his guilt the prosecution had to show that he intended to remain permanently away from the Army. His persistent absence strongly suggested that he did not intend to return. Private Amass, however, gave various reasons why each time he especially wanted to be at home – just for the moment. The fact that, as soon as the police arrived at the place where he was living, he got out through a back window, he explained as being due to panic and a prejudice against the police. I need hardly say that I disposed of these pitiful defences with no difficulty at all and he was sentenced to a substantial term of imprisonment or detention. During the period while he was awaiting an escort to take him away, my commanding officer put him in handcuffs. I very respectfully protested against this.

'You can't keep a man in handcuffs, sir,' I said. 'It's illegal.'

'If I don't, he'll escape again.'

'Not if he's properly guarded, sir.'

'Well, we'll go and see him,' said the C.O.

So we visited Private Amass, who confirmed my view that he did not like wearing handcuffs. He described them as uncomfortable and limiting his movements.

'Now, look, Amass,' said the C.O. 'If I have those handcuffs removed, will you give me your word not to escape again?'

'Yes, sir,' said Private Amass simply.

I was impressed with his sincerity. If he'd said 'May I be struck dead if I do,' I would have warned the C.O. that he was not to be trusted, because such asseverations are normally the hallmark of a liar. (Incidentally, I am told that on one occasion a witness said, 'May I be struck dead if I'm telling a lie!' The next moment he collapsed on the floor. But he had only fainted. However, I cannot vouch for this story as I was not present.)

But Private Amass's 'Yes, sir' suggested to me, with all my knowledge and experience of witnesses, that he meant it and I said so to the C.O.

'All right. They can take off the handcuffs.'

They took them off and a few days later Private Amass left our battalion – not under escort but under his own steam – and, as far as I know, he was never heard of again.

That was my first exploit in the orderly room, but I survived it and eventually actually became adjutant.

Some time later, when the C.O. was on leave, a man was brought up on a charge before the acting C.O., who relied implicitly on me as adjutant to steer him safely through the legal channels. It was a bad case and he sent the man to detention. After he had been taken away, a horrible thought occurred to me:

'I'm afraid there's been a slip-up,' I said. 'You ought to have asked him if he'd take your award or have a court martial.'

The acting C.O. (who, I am glad to say, is still a friend of mine) said, I thought very moderately: 'You might have told me. What do we do now?'

'You'd better have him back and ask him.'

We had him back. 'Private X,' said the acting C.O., 'I ought to have asked you whether you would take my award or have a court martial. Which would you prefer?'

Private X thought for a moment. 'I'll have a court martial, sir,' he said. There was a pause. The acting C.O. looked at me. I looked straight in front of me. Eventually the prisoner was marched out.

'Now what?' asked the acting C.O.

'We're in a fix,' I said. 'If he's court-martialled, he can say he's already been tried by you. A man can't be tried twice for the same offence. If you send him to do his sentence, he could claim that it's illegal because he was never given the chance of a court martial.'

'Well, what do we do?'

'The only thing, as far as I can see, is for me to see him and to try and persuade him to accept your award.'

'But he says he won't.'

'I know. But if we tell him that you won't send him to detention and will only give him C.B., he might agree.'

'But he ought to get detention for this,' said the acting C.O. 'And so ought you, if I may say so,' he added.

'I'm very sorry,' I said, 'but there's nothing else to be done.'

'All right. Better go along and see him.'

So the sergeant-major and I visited Private X.

'Private X,' I said, 'supposing the C.O. were to reconsider your punishment, d'you think you'd accept his award then?'

'That depends, sir, don't it?' said Private X.

'It depends on what?' I said, though I knew very well what he meant.

'On what the award's going to be,' said Private X. 'I ain't unreasonable, sir,' he added; 'if you tell me, I'll tell you.'

'Well,' I said as airily as I could, 'undoubtedly a slight mistake has been made and I think it possible that in the circumstances the C.O. might substitute an award of C.B. But of course I can't bind him to it in any way.'

'He knows you've come to see me, don't he, sir?' said Private X.

'Well, yes, he does.'

'And he knows what you're going to say to me, sir?' he asked.

It occurred to me that Private X might have done very well at the Bar himself. After he had most respectfully cross-examined me a little further, he agreed to accept the C.O.'s award. So he was duly marched in again, asked the missing question and given a trifling punishment of five days' C.B. He saluted very smartly the next time I saw him in the battalion lines.

Well, everyone can make mistakes and I managed to live that one down too, but some time later an unpleasant situation arose in one of the companies. Someone was stealing. They knew who it was but they couldn't prove anything. 'He was too fly,' they said.

'Too fly,' I said to myself. 'We'll see who's too fly.' So I spoke to his company commander. 'Don't worry,' I said. 'You send him to battalion headquarters. Then we'll set a trap for him. I know all about these things.' So Private Y was duly transferred to battalion headquarters. I decided to give him a couple of days to allay any possible suspicion and then to set some simple trap. Everyone hates a man who steals from his comrades and I'd no compunction about it. But I knew that sometimes traps fail for lack of efficiency. There would be nothing like that in this case, I assured myself. I would deal with it personally. I knew the dangers and there would be no mistake. Unfortunately, however, on the very night that Private Y first slept at battalion headquarters the battalion safe was broken open and all the money taken. I at once arranged for at least a dozen men, including Private Y, to have their kits thoroughly inspected and searched but nothing traceable to the robbery was found.

'I had nothing to do with the safe business, sir,' volunteered Private Y. 'Why should you think I had?'

The question itself was almost a confession of guilt. No one had said a word to him about the safe.

'Everyone's been searched,' I said.

'Oh no they haven't, sir. Only me and them.'

'Well, there are twelve of you.'

'But why pick on me, sir? I ain't done nothing. I've only just come here. I didn't even know where the safe was. Anyway, what should I want to break it open for?'

Everything he said was the hallmark of the thief and he was obviously the guilty party, but we couldn't prove a thing against him. So I sent him back to his company at once with many thanks for the loan.

'I told you he was too fly,' said his company commander. 'Even for you.'

*

Soldiers, on the whole, distrust lawyers and I'm afraid that I entered the Army with a fairly low opinion of the brain-power in the higher ranks of the service. Unfortunately I found a certain amount to justify my opinion. For example, when we were awaiting Hitler's invasion, a divisional commander sent out an order to the troops under his command that in no circumstances was the formation known as extended line (or, when I was in the O.T.C. at school, extended order) to be used in his division. Although I was extremely bad at the use of

ground and cover, even as a layman I thought that the way in
which infantry should advance must depend upon the circumstances existing at the time: the nature of the ground, the
distribution of the enemy forces, the fire-power on each side
and so on. I was certainly right in my views about this order.
The divisional commander had presumably woken up one
night or, being unable to sleep, had spent the time putting on a
page of foolscap his views on the subject and eventually coming
to the ridiculous conclusion which was published to all of us. It
was just as well that England was not invaded while he was in
command.

The worst example of almost inconceivable stupidity I came
across in the North African campaign, when no less than a
corps commander issued the following order:

'All natives found in possession of British or Dominion
clothing or equipment will be shot.' Just that. In fact many
natives had such clothing, much of which had been acquired by
them from Germans or Italians who'd captured it in the 1942
retreat. And no doubt some New Zealanders had given away
clothing or equipment in exchange for favours shown to them
by natives. If such an order had been obeyed, hundreds of
friendly natives would have been shot without trial through no
fault of their own. Possession of one shirt or one pair of shorts
would have meant immediate death. I cannot believe that
anyone in the corps area obeyed that order. We certainly took
no notice of it in our battalion. It is, of course, conceivable that
some staff officer on the corps commander's staff was to blame
for issuing the command, but it's doubtful whether such an
order could have been issued without at least the sanction of the
corps commander.

But as against this sort of behaviour, which entirely confirmed my prejudice against the ability of high-ranking army
officers, my preconceived views eventually received a jolt from
which they have never recovered. That jolt was provided by
Field Marshal Montgomery, a man whom I, at first, thought to
be just another general but one who made rather more fuss
about it than others.

❈ Homage to Montgomery

In the spring of 1941, while we were stationed at Milstead, we were told that a new commander would arrive to take over the corps to which we belonged. His name was Lieutenant-General Montgomery and I was told that he had quite a big reputation. I was not particularly excited. Corps commanders were seldom seen by a mere battalion officer and had no noticeable effect on our lives. However, the new corps commander proceeded to make his presence felt almost as soon as he arrived. All the officers in my division, and I think the whole corps, were suddenly ordered to attend a talk by General Montgomery at a cinema in Maidstone. This was madness, we said. At a time when the Germans were able to concentrate the whole of the Luftwaffe against England, hundreds of officers, perhaps the cream of the corps of officers, were to be concentrated in one cinema. What a target. However, it was an order and we had to obey.

The cinema was full of officers, many of whom saw with expressed annoyance large notices with NO SMOKING on them. We had to be seated a considerable time before the conference was due to start, and I listened, I'm afraid not without a certain eagerness, for the sound of sirens which would, I hoped, make the conference stillborn. However, they never sounded and punctually at the advertised time the small figure of the new commander strutted across the stage and slowly took up his position in front of us. There was the usual hush. Then he spoke.

'Gentlemen,' he said, 'there will now be an interval of thirty seconds for coughing. Please get your coughing done during that period, so that you may be quiet while I am talking.'

When the half-minute was over, he began. First of all he thanked us for coming. I should never have thanked my platoon for falling in when they'd been told to do so. Montgomery then went on to say that he wished to get to know us and for us to get to know him and that he proposed that morning to give us his views on training and his general appreciation of the war situation. He proceeded to give them. I was bound to admit that he spoke fluently and well and without notes. His mannerisms were, of course, noticed at once, the most noticeable being his use of the words 'I would say', the deliberate repetition of words or sentences to give emphasis and the very slight tendency to pronounce r as w. Later on, many years after the war when he wrote a book, I wrote a short parody of the sort of speech he might have been expected to give on publication day. Here it is.

. . . So I wrote a book – I wrote a book. And I would say that, if you are writing a book, there is one essential quality that book must have. One essential quality. It must provoke. It must provoke. Now books have been written which have not that quality but no one reads them and I would say that it would have been very much better if they'd never been written. It would have saved time for the printer, time for the publisher and time for the bookseller. I would say that it would have saved a great deal of time, a very great deal of time indeed.

Now why must a book provoke? And what must it provoke? And how must it provoke? Like all great truths the answer to these questions is very simple. I would say that it is very simple indeed. First, why must it provoke? A book must provoke because that is why people read books. To be provoked – they read them to be provoked. Some people wish to be provoked in their minds, some in their hearts and some in their desires. But each reader wishes to be provoked in some respect. Otherwise he would not read. There is no doubt about it. He would not read at all unless he wished to be provoked. So all the great books, all the good books and all the books which people read provoke. And when I wrote my book I made sure that, in whatever respect it might fail, it would not fail in that way and I would say categorically that it has not. It *has* provoked. There will now be an interval of two minutes for coughing.

Not long after the conference at Maidstone the corps commander came to inspect us and the battalion was ordered to parade in close order for his inspection. We thought it absurd. Apart from the danger of an air attack, battalions did not parade in close order at that stage in the war. We were steeped in the idea of dispersion. If a subaltern had been seen taking his platoon for a march in threes he would have had things said to him which would have impressed themselves on his mind or, if they had not, he might have ceased to be a subaltern. There was worse than that. Army Council instructions issued early in the war directed that brasses should not be polished but should be allowed to become dull, the object being to prevent them from shining and giving positions away to observers from the air. It was the corps commander's order that we were to clean our brasses. It would have been tempting to persuade an intelligent private soldier to refuse most politely to obey the order, on the ground that it was contrary to the Army Council instruction, and, if punished, to appeal to the Army Council. However, I had sufficient sense to resist the temptation.

Accordingly, with brasses clean and in close order the battalion paraded and awaited the inspection.

The men were ordered to remove their head-dresses on Montgomery's direction so that he could better observe the state of their health. He shook hands with all officers, including me. After the inspection he came to the battalion headquarters and there he made slight headway towards overcoming my antipathy. This was due to his expressing appreciation of the scones which were offered to him. I had been responsible for the tea provided and I was prepared to accept it as a personal compliment. He was very pleasant at tea and chatted with all of us. My then C.O., who was a good judge of character, said to me afterwards: 'Whatever you say about him, you can see for yourself that he is making everyone under his command realize that he is their commander. Ordinarily a corps commander means nothing to the officers and men in the battalion. General Montgomery intends to mean a great deal and that is absolutely the right idea.'

It is now generally admitted, even by those who are not Montgomery fans, that the pains which he took to get to know his troops and to bring home to them that he was their commander were a substantial military asset. In ancient times, when armies were smaller, a general would parade himself on horseback in front of his troops and would exhort them to deeds of valour. He secured their confidence by his bearing, his actions on the field and his eloquence. Above all, he was frequently seen by his soldiers. In modern armies in the field it is quite impossible for generals to parade themselves in front of more than a very small number of the troops. Even then, all that is seen by the average soldier is a glimpse of the general moving in a jeep or a tank. Yet it is as essential today as it was of old for men who are actually doing the fighting to believe wholeheartedly, not only in the cause for which they are fighting, but in the commander of the army in which they are fighting. Tanks do not drive themselves nor guns fire themselves. The men in or behind them must be just as confident as the infantry soldier going into the attack.

While with my battalion I met Montgomery at least five times to speak to personally. I never rose above the rank of major and on four occasions when I met him I was only a subaltern or a captain.

Before any battle Montgomery used to issue a message to all the troops under his command. This message was to be read out just before the battalion went into action. It was a most effective message and, after it had been read out, the troops went into action laughing at the ease with which their immediate objective could be attained. There is no doubt that Montgomery inspired complete confidence in them.

On one occasion when we were in the desert, I think it was before the Battle of Alamein, I was given a sealed envelope containing these messages which were to be read out at a particular time later on. On our way up to our battle positions we rested on a bit of sand and I left the envelope there. About two hours later I suddenly realized what I had done. I experienced the sort of emptiness which I had felt when I saw that Fortune was going to leave me alone to face a judge in the High Court. I had no excuse of any kind for my carelessness and, although I was on good terms with my C.O., he was slightly older than I was and was a regular officer and must have been aware by this time of my somewhat condescending attitude to the military establishment. Apart from my fears for my own personal position – which were considerable – I knew the effect of reading out these messages to the troops before a battle. I was distressed at the idea that we should not have the benefit of them on this occasion. However, I had to have a try to recover the messages, though I doubted whether it was possible. I went to a despatch rider and asked him if he could remember where we had been two hours previously and whether he could find the spot. If he did so, would he kindly find and bring back an envelope which I hoped he would see there. Fortunately he was a countryman who was as good at observing features on the ground, even in the desert, as I was bad. Off he went and in due course came back with the envelope. My relief was much the same as when Fortune had returned in time to deal with a difficult aspect of the case with which I had been left.

My C.O. never learned of my carelessness at the time, but years after the war I mentioned it when I was making a speech at a gathering of the branch of the British Legion of which he was President. At that meeting I also related an incident between us which had happened after some battle. I had had a conversation with him, the result of which was to make me very angry. In consequence of that I charged over a minefield in my carrier or jeep and really didn't care whether I was blown

up or not. My C.O. had seen this. Later on all he said to me
was:

'You know, Harry, we can spare you, but we can't spare the
transport.' Fair comment.

*

My battalion was part of the 131st Infantry Brigade and this
brigade was the lorried infantry in support of the armour in the
7th Armoured Division. In the Battle of Alamein our brigade
had been part of the 44th Division but, owing to large casualties,
this division was broken up after that battle and we were sent
to join the 7th Armoured Division. In this division the battalion
remained until the end of the war. After Alamein we moved
forward and took part in the battles for Tripoli, Mareth and the
Wadi Akarit.

Just before the battle for Tripoli I was very lucky, because
my C.O. and the second-in-command being slightly ill I
attended General Montgomery's conference with his commanding officers before the battle. The confidence which he inspired
in everyone under him was fantastic. After he had given out the
plan, I remember him saying:

'I would say that we will be in Tripoli by the 21st or, if you
like, the 22nd of January.'

We were in fact there on the 23rd of January. No one could
cavil at that.

Eventually we came to the Enfidaville line which was
immensely strong and of very great depth. The plan made by
the higher commanders for the final battle in the North African
campaign was as follows.

The Eighth Army was to make a fairly strong attack on the
Enfidaville line with the object of drawing off the German
reserves and without any actual intention of getting through the
line. Forty-eight hours after that attack had started, the First
Army was to attack from Medjez-el-Bab, proceed along the
valley, capture Tunis and thereafter clear the Cape Bon
peninsula.

The plan seemed sound enough. The Enfidaville line could

only have been forced – if at all – at the cost of tremendous casualties and there was only one route by which the armour and the transport could go through it. They would be under fire from the German guns the whole way and by the time the Eighth Army had completed its task of taking the line, it would probably have almost ceased to exist as an army. It would certainly have been incapable of any further effort without large reinforcements of men and materials. On the other hand, the enemy had a very strong respect for the Eighth Army and were bound to treat any attack by it as a really serious matter. It did in fact transpire that General Messe, who was in command of the enemy forces in that sector, had orders to hold the Eighth Army at all costs.

The country from Medjez-el-Bab to Tunis was suitable for armour and the not very difficult task of the First Army would have been made still easier if the Germans could be induced to throw in their reserves to stop the feint attack of the Eighth Army. Unfortunately, however, before the First Army attack was due to go in, the Germans themselves put in an attack on that army and, although it did not make much headway, they appeared to have disorganized the First Army's own attack. At any rate, when it was put in, it was a complete failure and only resulted in the loss of quite a number of tanks.

The position then was quite serious. The First Army had failed in their objective, the Eighth Army, although it had done what it had been ordered to do, was very far indeed from breaking through the Enfidaville line. At that moment (so I was later told) our commanders had been informed by the statesmen that Tunis must be taken at all costs within ten days.

The next we knew in my battalion was that a new plan was put into action by which the glory of taking Tunis and clearing North Africa was to be given to the Eighth Army. It was to break through the Enfidaville line.

I have already pointed out what a task this would have been and I may add that it would not have been much use achieving it unless the Army would remain strong enough to act offensively when the line had been broken. Nevertheless this was the order given and my battalion actually moved to a concentration area waiting for the word to be given to go forward in pursuance of this plan.

This much I know of my own knowledge because my battalion actually received the orders. I cannot pretend that any of us from the C.O. downwards liked the idea. We had taken part in mountain battles before, in particular the battle for Mareth and the Tarhuna pass. The Enfidaville line was far stronger than either of those. At that stage there was an interview between General Montgomery and General Alexander. Naturally I cannot say of my own knowledge what took place between them but I have been told, I think it was by General Horrocks, that at that meeting Montgomery said that he would carry out the orders if required but that he could not guarantee what state his army would be in at the end of the battle. I further believe that it was he who suggested that, instead of that plan being put into force, the 7th Armoured Division and the 4th Indian Division should be sent round to reinforce the First Army and that the attack on Tunis should then be made again along the valley from Medjez-el-Bab. That this was how it happened I cannot say for certain, but I do know that we were greatly relieved when suddenly our orders were cancelled and we were told that we were going round to join the First Army.

Had the plan not been changed it is very doubtful if I should now be writing this book. As everyone knows, the new attack was completely successful. Tunis was taken and the North African campaign was over.

One of the most exhilarating feelings is to rescue a country from its oppressors. I would have had to be very unemotional indeed not to be affected by the welcome we got from the inhabitants.

The 1st/7th Queen's were the first infantry to enter Tunis but we were sent on to clean up beyond. While we were in the process of doing this, it was a little galling for me to have a complaint made to me by a farmer that some of my troops had stolen a chicken. He was very angry.

'*Les Allemands étaient corrects,*' he said.

E

I took a lot of trouble to restore friendly relations and I think that in the end I succeeded.

If what I have written is correct, we owe a much greater debt to Field Marshal Montgomery than any of the military historians have stated. Because, if he was responsible for the change of plan for the capture of Tunis, it was he who was equally responsible for the shelving of a disastrous plan which would probably have resulted in the decimation of the Eighth Army and the consequent prolongation of the war for a considerable period.

After the fighting was completely over, we were sent back to rest at Homs and it was there that Thomp sent me to hospital. With the best of intentions he had rigged up a tent for me, the canvas of which was supported by a tall, heavy iron bar which he had somehow or other driven into the sand. During the night a wind blew up and the iron bar crashed on to my head. I woke up in hospital and that was the end of my combatant service with the Army.

⌘ The Second String

I came out of the Army in August 1945 and was back in practice again at the Bar in October. I was one of the lucky ones, because I had been practising long enough before the war to make it comparatively easy for me to pick up my practice again. But young men, who had only started five or six years before the war, lost everything by leaving the Bar for one of the Services.

Naturally I did not know it at the time, but in fact I was only going to practise for less than four years before I became a County Court judge. Within a short time of restarting practice I became very busy.

In 1948 Lettice became extremely ill and was found to have cancer. I immediately asked to be considered for a County Court judgeship, so that I should have as much time as possible with her. On 1st September 1949 I became a County Court judge and, in spite of her illness, I did have nine very happy months with her until she died in May 1950. I am most grateful for the happiness which she gave me during the short fourteen years of our marriage.

At that time County Court judges were extremely badly paid. My income went down to a little over £2000 a year. A County Court judge then received £2000 for his work as a County Court judge and, in addition, a few hundred pounds for sitting as a Divorce Commissioner.

Not very long afterwards the salary was raised to £2800 a

year, but this was to include the work as a Divorce Commissioner. Gradually the salaries of County Court judges were improved and today a Circuit judge receives £13,000 a year.

The status of County Court judges has also been improved. When I was appointed, the appointment was entirely in the hands of the Lord Chancellor and I was not required to take any judicial oath. Some years later the position was upgraded so that every judge was appointed by the Crown and required to take a judicial oath.

One rather odd thing occurred when the appointment of County Court judges started to be made by the Crown. Up to then the Lord Chancellor could remove a County Court judge for 'inability or misbehaviour'. As the Lord Chancellor had appointed the judge, it was reasonable that the Lord Chancellor should have the right to remove him. But, even after the appointment was placed in the hands of the Sovereign, the Lord Chancellor still retained the power to remove him without receiving the Sovereign's permission. And this is still the case.

*

My work as a professional author began at the same time as my work as a judge but had its origin much earlier in my life; I will deal with it first.

Although I started writing when I was a small boy, did a little at school and rather more at Cambridge, I had no time to learn to write professionally until my appointment as a judge. From then on I was able to follow both professions, though at one time I became a little anxious lest my responsibilities as a judge might conflict with my work as an author.

I have a fairly vivid imagination and have always enjoyed writing, my earliest efforts being in not very promising verse. Here are the first lines of one of my six-year-old efforts:

> There was a boy who slept all night
> But never went to bed.
> And when he got up he lost his pipe,
> So he smoked the match instead.

Although I shiver at the so-called rhyme of 'night' and 'pipe', I am sorry to say that this would pass muster in many popular songs, and, worse still, in Hymn No. 550,[1] where the author rhymes 'farthest' with 'regardest'.

I had improved a bit by the time I was twenty and I wrote a song for the *Bedder's Opera* for which Brian Davies wrote the music. André Charlot nearly accepted it for one of his revues. He wrote to say that he liked it and might be able to use it, but subsequently, after many reminders, he said that unfortunately the actor to whom he had given the script had lost it. Apparently André Charlot was not sufficiently interested in it to want another copy.

Brian Davies and I took it to Davy Burnaby, who had been a member of the Footlights and was at the time starring in the *Co-Optimists*. He was extremely nice to us, but, having read the lyric, he said that he was afraid that the last verse was too risqué for the West End. Davy Burnaby was anything but a prude and his comment shows how times have changed. Here is the complete song:

> A proctor's[2] cares lie on my head
> My labours are so great.
> I often wish that I were dead,
> But, failing that, I'd state:
> > I wish I were a pensive cow
> > I do.
> > If I could change, I'd do it now
> > And moo, moo, moo.
> > I'd wander through the grassy leas
> > As slowly as I could,
> > I'd sit and ruminate at ease,
> > I would, I would, I would.
>
> Although my countenance is stern,
> I love a harmless jest.

1. *Hymns Ancient and Modern*: Revised Edition.
2. Or 'doctor's' or 'parson's' or whatever.

Perhaps you'd be surprised to learn
A life I'd lead with zest.
  I wish I were a gentle stream,
  I do.
  I'd laze about all day and dream
  Of you, you, you.
  And when you crossed me in your boat,
  Although it might seem rude,
  I'd tip you out and watch you float,
  I would, I would, I would.

Within this breast there lives a heart
That yearns for spritely youth.
Alas I play an old man's part,
Although to tell the truth
  I wish I were a bright young boy
  I do.
  I'd find the sweets that never cloy
  For two, two, two.
  I'd take you to a dance one night,
  At first I'd be so good,
  But after supper – yes, you're right,
  I would, I would, I would.

When I was five or six I invented a little world of my own, which I called My Field. The inhabitants of my field were Mrs Fleeman, Mrs Deeman and Mrs Toboggan. I wish I could remember some of their antics and could describe, for example, how Mrs Fleeman and Mrs Deeman were indulging in mortal combat when Mrs Toboggan ran them over and decapitated both. But perhaps it is as well that I cannot remember a single one of their activities. I mention them because I think that they are possibly in line with the unlikely events which take place in some of my novels. The basis of many of my stories is the occurrence of an extremely improbable event, followed by completely logical action by all the characters in the story.

From the time I went to the Bar, however, I had no time for

writing, except for the articles on motoring law. But when I went into the Army, I found that my fellow officers seemed to be interested in the stories that I invented about the law.

'This is the sort of thing you could do,' I would say, and would then show how the law could be used or circumvented to provide the person who was using or circumventing it with amusement or profit or both.

Later on, when we were sailing for the Middle East, I told stories to the troops in serial form in an effort to entertain them. We had to go round the Cape, as we were not in command of the Mediterranean, and our voyage took a full two months. So every evening for some weeks I started a serial story which for the most part I made up as I went along, and at the end of the voyage I should say that I had probably told about seven or eight stories. None of them was in writing. Later on, when I was convalescing from the knock on the head provided for me by Thomp, I reduced them into writing and added some more. I had no knowledge of the literary market in those days, but I felt reasonably sure that it would be very difficult for a completely new author to sell a book of short stories. So I wrote a sort of link-up in the manner of *The Arabian Nights*, so that, although each story was completely different, the book was a complete whole. It was about a professor who went slightly mad as the result of a knock on the head and, instead of lecturing to students, told them stories. He was eventually certified but managed to escape from the hospital where he was detained. That part of the book which does not consist of the separate stories gives an account of the professor's exploits.

Someone typed it out for me in the Middle East and under the title *Full Circle* I sent it to Lettice, suggesting that she should send it to Macmillan. Macmillan thanked her very much and sent it back. After that she sent it to a few more publishers, all of whom sent it back without a word of encouragement. I then suggested to Lettice that she should put it away and that we should deal with it again when I came home.

After my return I tried a few more publishers and then put it away again. I was much too conceited to write for myself

alone. I knew that, although my style might improve a little if
I went on writing, I could not do anything substantially better
than *Full Circle*. Accordingly if no one was going to publish it,
I was not going to write any more.

The strong probability is that the book would never have
been published and that I should not have become an author if
my father had not collected stamps.

In 1922 my parents took a furnished house in Woking for the
summer. By chance there lived in Woking another stamp
collector who was known to my father. As a result I met his
daughter and she had a great friend called Petronella (Peter)
Burton. Peter had a younger sister of twelve called Naomi.
Naomi used to write to me from school and we continued to
correspond until she was grown-up. In 1939 she went to the
U.S.A. and joined the American branch of Curtis Brown, the
literary agents.

In 1946 Naomi Burton came to England for a holiday. She
had mentioned to me from time to time her friend Juliet O'Hea,
who was in the English office of Curtis Brown. Just before she
went back to the United States I thought I would have one
more try with *Full Circle* and I asked Naomi to introduce me to
Juliet. She did so.

Juliet read the book, suggested that I should substitute two
other stories for two stories which she did not think were in
keeping with the rest and, although she knew the number of
publishers who had rejected it, she said she thought she ought
to be able to place it. In fact, after several near-misses, she
placed it with Chapman & Hall, who were the seventeenth
publishers to have read it.

Since the publication of *Full Circle* Juliet O'Hea has assisted
me in my literary work to a fantastic extent and such success as
I have achieved in that field is to a large extent due to her
efforts. She has constantly advised me both about the actual
work itself and about its marketing, and very rarely indeed has
she been found to be wrong. Her reliability is one of her outstanding qualities and I shall always be grateful to her.

I hope that my experience will be an encouragement to new

authors not to despair or to give up if publishers refuse their first book. My actual writing has improved perhaps a little, but the substance of what I write has not.

I should also warn new authors not to expect too much from the publication of their first book. It is a great occasion when it actually appears and I believe that most authors expect (and I certainly expected) to see it on all the bookstalls and in all the shops. I lived near Paddington Station at the time it came out and on the day of publication I rushed round to the bookstalls expecting to see it in its dozens. It was nowhere to be found. The truth of the matter is that there is such an overwhelming number of books published that it is physically impossible for a copy of each book to appear on the bookstalls. And unless and until an author has acquired some kind of reputation or unless a particular book is a big hit new authors must be prepared for many disappointments.

My second book, *The Painswick Line*, I wrote just after Lettice had died. I was feeling utterly miserable but decided to fill up my time as much as possible. It is impossible for the ordinary person to think of two things seriously at the same moment. It is natural for a person who has lost someone dear to him to want to devote the whole of his time to grief. But, if you can make yourself do something which requires you to think, you will find that you cannot grieve at the same time. You must try to do something which requires the active exercise of your mind. Sewing mailbags won't do. Although I felt very far from light-hearted, I wrote what many people think is my most cheerful novel.

It was about the law, the church and the racecourse. Admittedly I introduced into it scenes which Lettice would have enjoyed. For example, the rectory in the book is a picture of the rectory at Kingsdown. But such episodes represented only a tiny proportion of the book.

I can't pretend that *The Painswick Line* was well put together. The story was partly about a clergyman, who was brilliant at picking winners, though he never made a bet himself.

In his genial review of the book, Lionel Hale wrote:

The novel . . . is entirely unscrupulous in the matter of shape. (The parson has a much better idea of form than his author.)

I hope that as a result of what Lord Justice Scrutton said to me I became less repetitious in my profession as an advocate, but I rather fear that, if I were charged with continuing to be unscrupulous in the matter of the form of my books, I might be in much the same position as the late William Cooper Hobbs who was most certainly unscrupulous in far more important matters. When he came up once again for sentence at the Old Bailey, the then Recorder of London said to him: 'Hobbs, you grow older but no better.'

Chapman & Hall published four more of my books after *The Painswick Line* and occasionally I actually saw one of them in the shops or on the bookstalls.

*

At about this time Richard Gordon wrote *Doctor in the House*. This was an immediate success and large numbers of copies were to be seen all over the place. When I went down to Paddington Station to see if my latest book was on show, I might occasionally find a dozen copies of *Doctor in the House* and, nestling modestly behind them, one copy of my new book. Richard Gordon's triumph with *Doctor in the House* gave me the idea of trying to do for the legal profession what he had done so successfully for the medical. I shall always be grateful to Richard Gordon for giving me the idea, but I should make it plain that my success has been trivial compared with his.

One of the publishers who had turned down my first book was Michael Joseph Ltd, and the director responsible for refusing it was Bob Lusty (now Sir Robert Lusty) who, in spite of this aberration, was to become a close personal friend of mine. At any rate, in his letter refusing it he did say some encouraging things about the book, which was more than any of the other rejecting publishers had done. But Bob was to do much more than this for me.

I offered the book to Chapman & Hall but only on terms as to advertising which they did not feel that they could accept.

Juliet then offered it to Bob, who not only expressed great
pleasure at the idea of publishing it but suggested the perfect
title – *Brothers in Law*. That was nearly twenty years ago and
radio versions of the book are still being broadcast, while the
book and many of its successors are still on sale in hardback and
paperback.

Within three weeks of publishing the book Michael Joseph
had sold more copies of it than the total sales of all my previous
six books put together. A great deal of the credit for the book's
success was due to Bob's flair as a publisher and the salesman-
ship of their brilliant sales manager (now managing director of
Heinemann), Charles Pick. I am most grateful to the late
Michael Joseph for his enthusiasm and advice, and to his widow
Anthea, who since Bob left the firm and her husband died has
been as attractive, understanding and intelligent a publisher as
any author could wish for.

When Bob left Michael Joseph and went as chairman and
managing director to Hutchinson, I found that I had divided
loyalties. Bob had become a great friend of mine. Michael
Joseph, the firm, had made a great success of my books. I solved
the difficulty by keeping with Michael Joseph for my novels and
going to Hutchinson for my serious books.

*

In the course of the past twenty years I have written thirty-
three books, and many radio plays, some based on my books and
some original. I have also written or collaborated in writing a
number of television plays and six plays for the stage.

The most successful of the plays for the stage was taken from
a book of mine, *Alibi for a Judge*, and was dramatized by me in
collaboration with Felicity Douglas and her husband Basil
Dawson. Andrew Cruickshank played the lead and it ran for
nearly two years at the Savoy Theatre. Andrew Cruickshank
is a remarkable man. He is a brilliant actor of great versatility,
but I doubt if there is any other prominent actor who could
also have become, if he had chosen, a professor of philosophy or
a bishop.

I wrote under my Christian names of Henry Cecil, but, had I ever thought that there was the slightest chance that I should become known as a writer, I would not have used this well-known family name.

In December 1952 I received the following letter:

Dear Cousin Henry!

I feel I must address you in this familiar manner because the holders of the name of Cecil form rather a limited clan, among which those bearing the Christian name of Henry are very rare – in fact I thought I was almost unique.

I should like to thank you very much indeed for the high literary esteem in the eyes of my friends to which your very excellent works have raised me.

As the recipient of very numerous congratulations on my happy facility with the pen and my astonishing grasp of the law for a mere naval officer, I should feel little less than a fraud if I did not pass them on to you – which I do now with my best wishes for Christmas.

Yours sincerely,
HENRY CECIL

This was from a genuine member of the Cecil family, a retired naval officer who was a son of Lord William Cecil. Eventually I got to know Henry Cecil, who was a delightful man of many talents. He wrote and composed but was extremely modest about his own achievements. I am sorry to say that he died some years ago. Since then, however, my wife and I have kept up with his charming widow, who has kindly given me permission to publish his letter.

When I looked up Henry Cecil's letter for the purpose of including it in this book I was surprised to find that it was written such a comparatively long time before *Brothers in Law* was published in 1955. I thought that few people had heard of me as a writer before the publication of *Brothers in Law*.

The film which the Boulting Brothers made of it and which was released in 1957 did a lot more to make my name known as a writer and, in consequence, all my previous books were reissued by Michael Joseph in hardback, while most of them were also published by Pan and Penguin.

In my apologetic reply to Henry Cecil I wrote that it was too late for me 'to go back now', i.e. either to use my real name or another pseudonym. But after the film had been shown successfully and subsequent books of mine published, I did start to worry lest a litigant in Willesden County Court who lost a case might, if he knew my identity, say or think in his disappointment that I didn't really try the case properly but was merely looking for material for my books. This would have been quite untrue, but, had anyone said it, I should have felt obliged to resign my judgeship. It is absolutely vital that litigants should trust the judge to try their cases according to the evidence and arguments before the court and that he should not be thought to be affected directly or indirectly by any other factor and, least of all, by any personal motive. Fortunately for me, no litigant ever said or suggested this and no one in the legal profession or outside it ever complained that it was unsatisfactory for me to adopt the dual role. But I could well have understood it if somebody had done so.

I was pleased that nobody did and I was particularly glad on one occasion that the Lord Chancellor's Permanent Secretary in addressing the County Court judges after a dinner started off his speech by saying, 'Your Honours – or may I say brothers in law'. This certainly gave me confidence that I was doing nothing objectionable. All the same I still worried about it and eventually I did try to start again.

I wrote a new book of much the same quality as the others and I arranged with a very old friend of mine to submit it to my agents under a new pseudonym. This pseudonym was Clifford Maxwell. My friend's second Christian name was Maxwell and this would naturally make anyone assume that he was the real author. The only people I took into my confidence were Juliet O'Hea and the Inspector of Taxes. The book was duly submitted to Michael Joseph Ltd, who strongly suspected that I was the author. When challenged with this, I didn't dispute it but asked them how they could be sure that it was not in fact a joint effort. Naturally they only paid a very small advance on publication of the book – less than one-tenth of what I usually received – and it eventually appeared. It was a failure, although I am sure that it was no worse than any of my other books. In consequence, I was simply unable to go on writing books under that name. I could not afford to do so. I had to pay tax on the money I had received in respect of the other books and it would have been financially suicidal to accept an advance of less than a tenth of what I was usually paid. This episode shows how important it is for an author to retain any goodwill which he may have acquired.

Writing books brings one into contact with other authors and one of my happiest experiences was meeting Dame Edith Sitwell, who became a friend.

One day the manager of the bookshop in Harrods telephoned to me to ask whether by any chance I had a spare copy of *No Bail for the Judge*. He said that he wanted it for Dame Edith. I was delighted at the thought that she wanted to read one of my books and I said that I would give her one with pleasure. The manager wanted to pay for it, but I said that I preferred to give it. I imagine that most authors would have been delighted to do the same. As a result, Dame Edith gave me one of her books and Harrods also presented me with a book, but, far better than this, my wife and I met Dame Edith and became firm friends.

Her choice of language was a never-ending source of joy. She was trying to write poetry when she was staying at the Sesame Club but was very much impeded by the fact that Messrs Longman, the publishers, who owned the premises next door, were doing considerable alterations to those premises and these included the installation of some lifts. They made a lot of noise in the process. I happened to know the manager of the Publications Department at Longman, who was a churchwarden at our church in Putney. I said that I would ask him if anything could be done to improve matters, and I did so. Subsequently she thanked me and said that the noise was 'much better now, only like giant mice superintending shipbuilding'.

*

People sometimes ask me what were the most important or thrilling moments in my judicial and writing careers.

The most important moment in connection with my becoming a judge was when I received a letter from Lord Jowitt's Permanent Secretary offering me the position. I was overjoyed, as this meant that I should now have plenty of time to be with Lettice.

The most thrilling moment in my other career was when I first heard my words spoken by professional actors and actresses. This was on radio. Nesta Pain, the author and brilliant B.B.C. producer, had read *The Painswick Line* and asked me if I would write a feature programme for her. I readily agreed. I called it *Mr Justice Faversham*. It was not very good, but Nesta assembled an excellent cast to appear in it. I still remember the intense pleasure which I had during the production.

I may say that the version which Nesta produced was not the original version which I had written. I had never written a radio script before. The first version made all the mistakes which a new radio writer can make and probably a good many more. When Nesta read it she said, in her disarming way:

'I think it's fascinating. Fascinating. But,' she added, 'there are just one or two things which I'd like to have a word with you about.'

By the time she'd finished having a word with me about the script, there was very little of it left. But she explained my mistakes so clearly that apparently I was able to avoid making most of them in the second version.

I have enjoyed attending the first nights of my plays, but I have always found that you cannot repeat a thrill of this kind and I have never had the same experience at a first night as I had at the broadcast of my first radio programme.

I very much enjoyed and enjoy my association with publishers, members of the B.B.C. and with actors and actresses. Members of the theatrical profession are, I suppose, among the kindest and most generous of people. There is only one rule which an author has to observe in talking to them and that is never to criticize their performances in any way, except, of course, by way of praise. Any adverse criticism which he wishes to make or any alterations which he wishes a member of the cast to make in the way the lines are spoken he must attempt to achieve through the director. I became well aware of this at a production by Nesta Pain of someone else's work. She, as she subquently admitted, somewhat ill-advisedly invited the author to address the cast. He criticized them, sometimes favourably and sometimes unfavourably. If they had been cannibals they would have eaten him, and it seemed to me that in the circumstances they preferred his blame to his praise. Nesta told me she would never do such a thing again and it was an object lesson to me.

I once wrote an article called 'I haven't changed since I was eight' and I think that this is true, although I hope that I have learned by experience to make my worse faults less obvious. But I was a mischievous small boy and it was this sense of mischief that impelled me to speak to the leading lady in a play of mine at one of the very early rehearsals, when I hardly knew her. She was a very lovely and gifted actress but I had no doubt at all that she would not expect to be told by me how to play the part. During a rehearsal I took the opportunity of asking her whether I could have a word with her at the next break. She smiled charmingly and said: 'Yes, of course', but in spite of the charming smile I realized that, as I had intended, she expected that my intention was to ask her to say certain lines differently or something of that sort and that the prospect of that did not exactly please her. When the time came I took her aside and said that all I wanted to say was that she was absolutely superb in the part. And indeed she was.

Sometimes I may appear to cut women friends of ours, particularly if they are attractive. This is simply because I have an extremely bad memory for faces – I see with my ears – and do not like to appear to be trying to pick up good-looking women in the street. My second wife, Barbara, and I were once staying in a very comfortable hotel in Wales and we had become quite friendly with the proprietors. One day there came to the hotel a pleasant-looking middle-aged man, who was accompanied by a boy of about twelve. He was a very affable fellow and most of us got to like him. We particularly noticed how considerately and helpfully he treated the small boy and we soon christened him 'Jolly Uncle'. All went well until, after about a fortnight, Jolly Uncle and the small boy disappeared in the very early hours of the morning with their luggage. The proprietors had not been paid a penny.

Not so long afterwards Barbara and I were having coffee at a Lakeland hotel where we had been staying for a day or two, when I saw the manager of the hotel coming out of the restaurant with a man.

'Look,' I said to Barbara, 'there's Jolly Uncle. I'm not going to let him get away with it again.' And I made ready to get up and go and speak to the manager. But I was saved the trouble of getting up, because the two of them came over to our table.

'Judge,' said the manager, 'I thought you might like to meet your colleague, the judge of the Kendal County Court.' I never told the manager how grateful I was to him for preventing me from dropping a very considerable brick, but I wonder which of the two men I would have picked out if both Jolly Uncle and the Kendal County Court judge had been on the same identification parade.

I haven't a good memory for faces, but even those who have are often unable to place a person whom they see out of context. For example, at a cricket match you may sit next to a man whose face you feel sure that you know but you can't think who he is. He happens to be the booking clerk who frequently supplies you with a ticket, but you don't recognize him in the different surroundings. On one occasion a man appeared in front of me on a judgment summons. I knew his face and assumed that this was because he had appeared in front of me before on at least one previous occasion. So, when he said that he didn't realize the seriousness of the matter, I intervened and said:

'But, Mr X, surely you must have. You've been here before.'

'No, your Honour,' he said, 'never.'

'Will you swear that?' I asked. I felt certain that it couldn't be true.

'Certainly, your Honour,' he said.

My face must have shown my surprise. I couldn't believe that a man would swear that he hadn't been in court before, if he had been. The truth could be so easily proved. Yet how was it that I knew his face?

'We *have* met under other circumstances,' said the man.

And then I realized that he was an actor who had been appearing in a television series which I had collaborated in writing. I had seen him frequently and had even had drinks with him at the B.B.C. bar.

'I am sorry,' I said. 'I'm afraid I can't go on with your case. You will have to go before the other judge.'

⊞ Becoming a Judge

There are so many more judges today that it must be much less of a rarity to come across a judge than it was. There is no doubt that most people have a tremendous respect for judges, and it would be against human nature if some of us were not affected by this.

When I was first made a judge, Lettice was very ill and I took a furnished house in the country. There was no telephone. I asked the local telephone manager how long it would take before I could have one.

'Six months or more,' he said, 'unless you're a doctor.'

I said that I wasn't a doctor but that my wife was ill and I wanted to be able to talk to her during the day from court.

'From court?' he queried. 'Are you then a barrister or a solicitor?'

I said that I was a County Court judge.

'You will have a telephone tomorrow,' he said, and he kept his word.

About this time I wanted some food which my wife fancied and which was probably only obtainable at some shop like Fortnum & Mason. I had no account there. I telephoned them, told them of my wife's illness and asked if it would be possible to put the goods on a train. I was asked if I had an account and I said that I had not. The representative told me that he was sorry but that it was quite impossible. Then, as an afterthought, he asked me my name. I gave it, prefixed by the word 'Judge'.

'The goods will be sent today,' he said. 'I think we deliver in your district.'

Having thanked him very much I asked about payment.

'We'll open an account for you,' he said.

'Don't you want any references?' I asked.

'Certainly not.'

Both these events happened within a month of my becoming a County Court judge. I'm not sure that they were good for me.

The first thing I noticed about sitting as a judge was a complete absence of strain. As an advocate I was not only listening to every word that was said but I was turning over in my mind the whole time the possibility of furthering my case in one way or another. All the time I was looking for a chink in my opponent's armour. As a judge I had to listen to every word and I wanted to get the decision right but normally I did not mind which side won. I say 'normally' because judges are human and, when the law appears to be working against justice, there are few judges who do not strive to interpret the law so that justice may be done.

The average judge, unlike the advocate, is not working under continuous strain. There are exceptions like the late Mr Justice Slade, but I have found that most judges with whom I have discussed the matter had the same experience as I had. But listening to every word that is said is undoubtedly tiring and to do that for five hours a day, with an interval of an hour for lunch, is in my view as much as a judge can do satisfactorily. In the old days judges would sit incredibly late and, even in my own time, on assizes, judges sat far too late. This is unfair to everyone, particularly to the parties whose cases are being tried. Today late sittings are rare.

People sometimes complain about the long holidays which judges enjoy. Judges could get through their work somehow without any holidays at all, but the quality of their work would gravely deteriorate, and in particular the temper of many of them would suffer. It is difficult for a witness who is in court for the first time to give evidence before the kindest of judges, but to do so before a judge who bites his head off would not only be a humiliating experience but would not be likely to produce the best kind of evidence to lead to a fair decision in the case.

When I was a judge I took long holidays and I make no apologies for having done so. I say nothing about the quality of my decisions but I could never claim overtiredness as an excuse for giving a bad judgment or conducting a case in an unfair manner.

When I was first appointed I decided to model myself on Judge Snagge, who never said an unnecessary word. But, when later on I told my friends this, I had to add that I hadn't stopped talking since. However, although no doubt I intervened too often, I am glad to say that my interventions were not enough to be criticized in the Court of Appeal. Nevertheless I am sure that it would have been more satisfactory if I had said less. I should have had the words of verse 2 of Psalm 39 in front of me:

> I held my tongue and spake nothing; I kept
> silence, yea, even from good words; but it was
> pain and grief to me.

I would sometimes go into court determined to keep my mouth shut and even keep quiet for a full five or ten minutes and then something was said which required elucidation and I had to ask for it and, once having spoken, I could not turn back.

Not long after I had been appointed I was going by train to Windsor where I sat as a judge once a week. A young barrister with a blue bag got into my carriage. Apparently the clothes which I was wearing and the suitcase on the luggage rack above me suggested that I was going to the County Court.

'Are you going to Windsor?' he asked.

I said that I was.

'What's the judge like?' he asked. 'I've never seen him before.'

On this occasion I was able, after a split second's struggle, to subdue the sense of mischief which urged me to conceal my identity for a while.

'I'm afraid I'm prejudiced,' I said. 'It's me.'
That young man is now Mr Justice Bridge.

*

Earlier on I said facetiously that Judge Sturges would probably
have decided in favour of a horse. This reminds me of a case
which came before me when I was a judge. It was a claim for
possession of a house, the landlord was entitled to an order for
possession and the only question was how long I should give to
the tenant. Now in cases of this kind the jurisdiction of the judge
is strictly limited. I proposed to give the tenant what I considered to be the maximum time which I had the discretion to
allow, namely two months. The landlord's counsel objected. He
quoted one of the leading cases on the subject where a compassionate judge had made an order allowing six months to a
poor old man who earned his living as a rag-and-bone man and,
for this purpose, kept his horse in a stable. It was possession of
the stable that the landlord was seeking. When the judge gave
the old man six months in which to find other accommodation
for his horse, the landlord appealed and the judges in the Appeal
Court said that the order was wrong in principle. They sub-
stituted an order for possession in twenty-eight days. In the case
before me possession was sought of a dwelling house where
people were living and I said that, if a horse was entitled to
twenty-eight days, I thought two months was fair for human
beings.

Judges of County Courts have many cases where landlords
and tenants or neighbours are in dispute. Their quarrels are
often about trifling matters, but I can understand that, if you
are living next door to someone whom you cordially dislike, the
smallest lack of consideration on his part may give you a deep
sense of grievance. On a good number of occasions I would go
to the scene of the trouble, first of all to see what it was all about
and secondly to see if I could find a satisfactory solution to
avoid the necessity of applying strict law to the matter.

The parties were always delighted that I came to see for
myself. They obviously felt – quite rightly – that it was much

easier for me to see their points of view if I saw the actual hedge or washing line or dog or whatever the bones of contention were.

On two occasions my visits led to unexpected results. It is over three hundred years since an English judge accepted a bribe and nearly one hundred and fifty since one was offered. On that occasion a litigant sent Mr Baron Alderson £10 in the hope of obtaining a favourable decision. The judge was going to have the man prosecuted for contempt of court, but, on being told that the offender 'did it in ignorance', he contented himself with reprimanding the man and returning the £10 to him. Presumably Mr Baron Alderson treated the man as a sort of Rip van Winkle who had woken up to find to his surprise that bribery of judges had long since disappeared.

No one tried to bribe me, but some time after I had satisfactorily settled a dispute between neighbours, one of them wrote to me and said that he was so grateful to me for having pointed out to him, when I was at his premises, that he was really the person to blame for the trouble. He said that, in consequence, everything in his garden was now lovely and that there were no demons at the bottom of it. As an earnest of his gratitude he enclosed 10s for me to give to any charity of my choosing. I'm afraid that we had to return the money but we wrote him a nice letter.

In another similar case a woman wrote to me and said that I had shown such obvious fondness for animals, when I paid my visit, that she would be very pleased if I would accept as a present one of her dogs for which she wanted to find a good home. I had to refuse the kind offer but I hope that I did it graciously.

Judges, when at the Bar, are so used to witnesses going in and out of the witness-box that some of them do not realize, when they first begin to sit as judges, that for most witnesses it is a very unnerving experience to have to give evidence.

To begin with, they have to take a ridiculous oath which no conscientious man who believes in God can properly take. He is asked to say that he swears by Almighty God that the evidence he gives shall be the truth, the whole truth and nothing but the truth. The honest, intelligent man knows that, however sure he may be of his facts, his recollection may be wrong. He could easily swear that he would do his best to tell the truth but he is not allowed to do that. He has to swear to tell the truth, whether he knows it or not. One of the most frequent cases to come before the court is that of a road accident. The whole thing happened in a flash and, although an honest person's recollection may be right, it certainly may be completely wrong. Yet he is compelled to swear by his Maker, in whom he believes, that it will not be wrong. But worse is to come. He is also compelled to swear that he will tell 'the whole truth'. In many cases the laws of evidence will not permit him to disclose the whole truth. If a man who witnessed an accident went home and told his wife all about it, what he said to his wife would be very valuable evidence two years later as to whether his recollection of the accident was correct. But the law says that it is hearsay evidence and cannot be given. A religious man will consider his duty towards his God to be greater than his duty towards the court, though I must admit that I never encountered a witness who insisted on telling me what he told his wife, because otherwise he would be failing in his duty towards his God.

Finally, the witness is required to swear that he will tell nothing but the truth, when, once again, an honest and reasonable man knows that something that is not true may accidentally stray into his evidence.

It would be far more satisfactory if witnesses were required to swear or affirm that they would do their best to tell the truth, and if this oath or affirmation were administered by the judge standing up, as it is in Scotland. This could be done in quite as dignified and solemn a way as the oath is administered at present, and it would be an oath which the witness could keep.

First of all the witness has to go through the ordeal of taking the oath. Sometimes he has to do it several times because some witnesses insist on saying 'the Almighty God' or 'my Almighty God' instead of 'Almighty God'. A conscientious usher then makes him take the oath again. When he has got over that ordeal he then may hear as in a dream counsel saying to him, 'Now, Mr Jones, would you kindly cast your mind back to the 19th January 1972.' I should have thought that many witnesses at that stage haven't got a mind to cast backwards, forwards or sideways.

Before swearing the witness, the usher usually says:

'Are you a Christian?'

More than once the answer has been: 'I'm not a Christian. I'm a Roman Catholic.'

After I had been on the Bench some time I probably went too far in trying to make the witness as comfortable as possible. In the first place I offered him a seat. Many witnesses do prefer to stand, but, if they are going to be in the witness-box a long time, it is reasonable for them to be told that they can have a seat whenever they want it.

Then I would explain that the advocates and I all realized the difficulties of giving evidence and that we should quite understand if the witness's mind went blank. In that case he should say so and ask for a short interval in which to reorientate himself.

I had to be careful, however, that I did not upset the witness by too much kindness. For example, one man came into the witness-box in a state of tension and expecting everybody to question him severely. When I spoke in a kindly way to him before he'd been asked a single question, he simply burst into tears.

I do, however, think that it is important to put the witness at ease as far as can be done and to make his experience as little unpleasant as possible.

I think my attitude of mind in trying cases can to some extent be gauged from a letter which I once wrote to a litigant. I had tried an accident case and had found that both sides were to blame, though I do not remember in what proportions. There had been no serious personal injuries and it was not a case which I would have remembered had I not received a letter from one of the parties, who was a young student. He thanked me for the way in which I had tried the case but complained that not only was my decision wrong but that it had completely destroyed his faith in British justice. He added that the case may have done one good thing, namely that, as he had not yet made up his mind what career to adopt, he might decide to go to the Bar with the intention of bringing the law more into keeping with justice.

I would not normally correspond with a person who had appeared before me in a case, but I could see that the young man was really worried and so I decided to answer the letter. This is what I wrote:

Dear Mr ——,

You probably realize that it is not normally proper for a litigant to correspond with the judge who has presided at his trial, but I am answering your letter, not to discuss the case, which is of course out of the question but to try to prevent you from going through life with a sense of grievance or a belief that there is something basically unsound in the courts of this country.

As an intelligent young man you must realize that perfect justice is unobtainable by man. Most cases in this country are probably decided correctly but of necessity some will be decided wrongly, either because the judge makes a mistake or is deceived or there is another reason. Injustices are therefore bound to occur. When they do, they are bound to cause a sense of frustration in those who are adversely affected.

But the same kind of thing happens in every walk of life. It happens in the medical profession where a mistake or error of judgment may cost a person his life or cause grievous injury. It must happen in the teaching profession where a person may be wrongly ploughed in an examination and have his whole life affected. It happens on the roads where many thousands of people are killed and injured by mistakes.

Most of us at one time or another in our lives suffer disappointments, grief and even tragedy, sometimes through our own fault, sometimes through other people's and sometimes through sheer bad luck. If we are going to live sensible, useful and happy lives we have to accept the slings and arrows with as good grace as possible. You cannot be sure of winning in any walk of life, even though you are in the right. And when you lose you must make the best of it. If the partial loss of an accident case, where no one was badly hurt and where your character was not assailed and where the amounts involved were small, is going to leave you with a deep sense of the law's inadequacies I can only say that I should not recommend you to read for the Bar. The man who worries about cases unduly after they are over will not be a happy practitioner. In your early days at the Bar you will almost certainly lose cases which you ought to have won. Confidence in advocates is valuable, even necessary, but it is perhaps a little arrogant to think that (should you come to the Bar) you may be able to improve the standard of justice. It will always be imperfect, and if the worst it ever did is exampled in your case it has done pretty well.

I should make it plain that in saying what I have I am not intending in any way to comment on the correctness or incorrectness of my decision. I am confining myself to generalities, and trying to help you to see things in perspective, so that hereafter, whatever you do, you may lead the happy and sensible and useful life which I am sure is your aim. I do not want an answer to this letter but I hope it may be of some help to you.

I wonder how he got on. I would sometimes have liked to learn what happened to a person after a case but I took the view that a judge should not become involved in a case even after it is over, and, that being so, it was impossible for me to follow up the careers of people who have come before me.

If I had not taken that attitude, I should certainly like to have known what happened to a young man of eight who was the only witness of an accident and who gave evidence before me. In the case of young children a judge has to be satisfied that they understand what they are doing when they take the oath. Usually some question is asked about God or Heaven or Sunday School or something of that sort and they are then allowed to take the oath.

This is the exact dialogue that took place between me and this boy whose head hardly came above the witness-box.

I said to him: 'Do you know what is meant by telling the truth?'

'Yes.'

'What?'

'Not telling lies.'

'Why not tell lies?'

'Because it doesn't pay.'

'Why doesn't it pay?'

'Because no one would ever trust you.'

Readers may think that I was grossly unfair to ask such difficult questions but plainly I asked them of the right person. The young man had a very attractive mother in court and I should have liked to have asked them round to tea afterwards, but unfortunately such things can't be done.

This brings to my mind the way in which judges are supposed to behave. It is as important that they should be thought to behave well as that they should in fact behave well. And the only way of being sure that one is thought to behave well is by not behaving badly. For example, while I was a judge, I did not consciously exceed the speed limit. This necessity for good behaviour is sometimes a little inhibiting. I remember that one day, while I was a widower, the telephone rang in my flat. I answered it.

'Good morning. *Va bene?*' said an attractive foreign female voice.

'I beg your pardon?' I said.

'It is Angela, the little Italian girl,' came the voice. I knew no Angela of any dimensions and sadly I said that she must have the wrong number.

*

It was not because of my regrets for Angela that at the end of 1954 I married Barbara Ovenden. Once again I was extremely lucky and once again my wife came from the West Country. Barbara comes from Somerset and is a member of the R. D. Blackmore family. We are in the twenty-first year of our very happy marriage. I have a splendid stepson, who is a country doctor, a charming stepdaughter-in-law who is also a doctor, and three sweet little step-granddaughters, Sophie, Camilla and Emma. I cannot think of a better life than that of a happily married County Court judge, except that of a happily married retired County Court judge.

I now want to make the sort of digression which Lionel Hale no doubt had in mind when he criticized *The Painswick Line*.

Bob Lusty had told me that he started life as a publisher with Hutchinson in the days when Walter Hutchinson was in command of that firm. He had had a few months' experience as a reporter on a local paper and then, at the age of nineteen, he was given an interview with the great man himself. He obviously made a good impression, because at the end of it Walter Hutchinson took Bob along to another member of the firm with this introduction:

'This is Robert Lusty,' he said. 'He's a fully qualified journalist and will be of great use to you.'

I had a nephew by my second marriage, Simon Virgo, who was a very likeable and talented young man with an original mind and great strength of purpose. Barbara and I were very fond of him. He had been at Cheltenham College and, when he left school, he said that he wanted to become a publisher. Now it was not at all easy for a young man who had no university or literary qualifications to do this. Accordingly I advised his parents, who were very anxious for Simon to do what he wanted, that they should try to arrange for him to go as a reporter on a local paper, if necessary for no salary at all. Simon's father arranged this without difficulty. I told them that, when he had done six months on the paper, I would send him with a note of introduction to Bob. In due course I did this. Simon was then nineteen. The note said: 'This is Simon Virgo. He is a fully qualified journalist and will be of great use to you.'

I knew that Simon would make a good first impression and felt sure that Bob would find the form of the introduction irresistible. He was bound to think of himself thirty years previously in the same position at the same age. I was right.

Simon spent a year with Hutchinson and then did his National Service, most of it in Malaya. This gave him a taste for travel and when he came out of the Army he went round the world entirely by his own efforts, taking any job when it was necessary to provide for the expense of the journey. Eventually he joined Angus & Robertson, the publishers, in Australia. After some time with them and having learned Japanese, he went on to Japan where he was employed in Tokyo by Charles Tuttle for about five years. He did very well there but eventually decided that he wanted to come home. When he came home, he was for a short time with André Deutsch, but found that he did not like living in London. So he joined David & Charles in Newton Abbot, where he was very happy until tragically he was killed in an accident in 1972.

In the tiny, unusual, picturesque old Cotswold church in Syde, a small hamlet where his parents had lived for some years, they dedicated a stained-glass window to him, and Bob came to the ceremony and delivered a most moving address. It was typical of Bob's kindness to young people that he should have helped Simon throughout his career and that after his tragic end he should have taken part in this service to his memory.

*

I sometimes tell Barbara that I married her for lunch. I first became a permanent judge at Willesden in 1953. Until then I had been going there once a fortnight and on these occasions at lunchtime I used to go about a mile away from the court to an hotel. This was not very satisfactory, but, as it was only once a fortnight, I did not mind. Although I was not particularly overweight when I became a judge, my father had a tendency to put on weight, which I share. What I determined never to do was to adopt the practice of some County Court judges, who took sandwiches with them to court. Just as it is said that we spend most of our lives in bed, so it could be said that, if you have toast for breakfast and sandwiches for lunch, you spend most of your eating time eating bread. Even before I had complaints from my doctor about my weight, I was determined not to spend my time between bread and bed. So, when I came to Willesden in 1953, I asked the usher if he would go round the houses near the court and see if he could find anyone who would be kind enough to cook a meal for me at midday. He did this without much difficulty, but after a time the lady became ill and found it too much for her. I then found first one firm of caterers and then, when they gave up, another, who provided me with a proper lunch at the court. And when the second firm gave up, there was nothing for it and I married again.

Each day Barbara sent me to court with a Thermos flask of soup (note the capital 'T'), some cold meat and salad, some cheese and an apple. I am conservative in my habits and, although I have been retired now for seven years, I usually still have the same lunch. Barbara used to send sufficient soup, cheese and apples for the Registrar as well and, if another judge came to the court, she would send enough for him too. Sometimes I would bring a guest to the court who sat with me on the Bench. The Registrar said he always knew when it was a woman guest because then I had smoked salmon as well.

I refer to the Thermos flask because of a letter which I received shortly after my first book, *Full Circle*, had been published. It was forwarded to me from the publishers, and I felt sure that it must be a fan-mail letter – my very first. I opened it with some excitement. It was from the manufacturers of Thermos vacuum flasks complaining that I had spelt Thermos with a small 't' and saying in effect that, provided I didn't do it again, they would take no action this time.

*

A County Court judge has plenty of worthwhile work and quite enough legal points to satisfy his interest in law. At the same time he is dealing with very human problems and often has the opportunity of acting as peacemaker. It may well be that I did this too often, but I hope it was a fault on the right side.

When I tried a case between quarrelling neighbours I often used to suggest to them how much happier they would be if they could be on good terms with each other. I'm afraid that sometimes I used to make rather long speeches on the subject, pointing out, for example, how much more happily the day would start if a man left his front garden for work after a cheerful word or two with the man next door than after exchanging scowls. I usually said that I was on the best of terms with my neighbours and that it made life so much more pleasant. On one such occasion I was told that a solicitor's clerk was afterwards heard to say:

'I'd be on good terms with my neighbour if I knew that he was a judge.'

I've mentioned cases where it was possible for me as a judge to persuade the parties to settle the matters in dispute between them on fair and sensible terms without insisting upon the exact letter of the law being enforced. This is not always possible and after I had been a judge for some years I began to worry about the possible aftermath of the cases which I had decided. This was particularly so when debtors faced the possibility of going to prison unless they paid so much a week or so much a month, and in cases where people were being turned out of their houses or their rooms.

Many of the people concerned in these matters were inadequate and obviously had difficulty in communicating. As I said before, a judge cannot be concerned personally with what happens after a case has been decided, but it seemed to me that, where the party against whom an Order had been made was not represented by a lawyer, something should be done for him. In the magistrates' courts a probation officer is always available. In the High Court a person is normally represented by solicitors and counsel. It was only in the County Court that such people were left in what might seem to them to be a hopeless position.

Accordingly, when I was invited to address an organization of social workers, I made the suggestion to them that they should start a welfare unit and that a member of this unit should attend at my court or some other County Court and seek to assist, if only by a friendly chat, people who had got caught up in the law and did not really know what to do about it. The organization which I addressed said it was a very good idea and did nothing whatever about it. But the editor of the local newspaper also thought that it was a good idea and he wrote a leading article on the subject. In consequence, an accountant who was interested in politics came to see me and said that he himself, living in the neighbourhood as he did, would be prepared to carry out my suggestion. This was the origin of the welfare work which has been carried on at Willesden County Court and some other courts ever since. This accountant was followed by other people and finally by a member of the Institute of Directors, Mr Emil Wertheimer, whose devotion to this work while I was the judge and ever since must have done an immense amount of good.

At the end of a case, if I thought that either or both parties required some kind of assistance, I would ask them whether they would like to see the welfare officer and, if one of them said he would, I asked the other side whether they had any objection. There never was any objection and the welfare officer would then take the man or woman outside the court and talk to him or her. At the very least what this service provided was a feeling on the part of the man who was being assisted that he did have a friend in the world. But often much more could be done than that and, indeed, in one case I know that Mr Wertheimer was personally responsible for saving a man from losing a leasehold interest which was worth about £3000.

Although it is impossible to be a satisfactory judge if you worry overmuch about your cases and the results of them, you would not be human if on the way back from court to a comfortable home you did not reflect with some sadness on the condition of people who were so much less fortunate. And I have to admit that the welfare scheme was a personal advantage to me, in that I knew that the sad case of Mr Jones or Mrs Brown would be investigated by Mr Wertheimer who would show a most kindly, sensible and selfless interest in their cases.

I did, however, once have a case before the welfare scheme was introduced where I do not think that even Mr Wertheimer could have been of help.

Another judge had made an Order against a man to give up possession of a house in three months unless he complied with the repairing covenants in his lease. He failed to comply with them and applied to me for more time in which to carry them

F

out. On his application it became apparent that he would be quite unable to carry out the repairs owing to lack of means, but he said that he would carry them out himself and I gave him two months in which to do them. At the end of the two months, according to the landlords, he had still failed to do them and I decided to inspect the premises myself. The man was not represented and the landlords were represented by counsel. I drove the two of them to the premises in my car. It immediately became evident that the tenant, if not actually certifiable, was very close to being insane. Whenever I tried to talk on some neutral topic, such as the weather, he would only reply that he had written to all the members of Parliament and all the mayors in England and Wales that he was being persecuted and that no one would do anything for him. It was almost impossible to get a rational statement out of him. When I inspected the house, it was indeed a sorry sight. The tenant was a married man with children, but his wife had left him taking the children with her and also taking the furniture. There was nothing in the house at all except an iron bedstead on which there was an Army greatcoat. The premises were in a hopeless state of repair and it was obvious that the man could not conceivably put them right.

We went back to court and I tried to point out to the man that, however sorry for him I might be, the landlords were entitled to have the house kept in reasonable condition. He asked me for more time to complete the repairs himself. The landlords were receiving their rent from the National Assistance Board and, although I felt sure that he would be unable to complete the repairs himself, I saw no particular injustice in giving him a little extra time but I said to him that on this occasion, unless he did the repairs, I should have to give the landlords leave to issue a warrant to obtain possession.

'That will be quite unnecessary,' he said. 'I shan't be in this world if you make that Order.'

I made the Order giving him about another month and I instructed the court to notify the police, the local authority and any welfare association which was concerned with this area

But at the end of the month he committed suicide by drinking Jeyes' fluid. Before that, he had asked his wife to let him have the children for a day or two, but I am glad that she refused, because I strongly suspect that he would have murdered them. He had in fact been certified on at least one previous occasion and he was determined not to go back into a mental institution. It was a very sad case, but, although obviously it is not one I can forget, I have not allowed it to worry me unduly. It would be impossible for a judge to carry out his duties satisfactorily if he allowed the sad situations which he came across to depress him.

But because of this case I did on a later occasion with the best of intentions make one man very angry.

It was a case where I had held that a man was guilty of fraud and he had appealed. The Court of Appeal upheld the finding of fraud and he wrote to me saying that with this finding against him life was not worth living. Although such an expression is not necessarily to be taken at its face value, having regard to the other case which I have just mentioned, I did not want to take any risks. I instructed the Registrar to answer the man's letter in a suitable way, saying that unfortunately the judge could not enter into correspondence about cases which he had tried, but hoping that he would make up his mind to put the matter behind him. I then telephoned the welfare department of the local authority, told them what the situation was and asked whether a member of that department would be prepared to deliver the letter personally to the man, just in case in a fit of anger or despair when he received the letter he did something silly. At first the person I spoke to said they were not concerned with such matters. I said that it was perfectly all right but, should the man commit suicide, they might bear some responsibility for his doing so. In the end the department agreed to send someone with the letter. My fears were in fact wholly unjustified and the man was furious that it was thought necessary to send a welfare officer to him.

I know that some judges do not agree with the provision of the unofficial welfare service in the County Court. They say that the job of the County Court is to try cases and, once the cases have been tried, that's an end of the matter, except for the putting into force of any judgments. A judge, they say, must not become involved in the fate of either party in the case. I see this point of view, but I do not agree with it. Provided the judge has nothing whatever to do with the advice or actions taken by the welfare officer, it seems to me that it is not only perfectly proper but highly desirable that he should give the opportunity to one or other or both of the parties to consult someone who may be able to help them after the case is over. I cannot see the difference between this situation and that which obtains in a magistrates' court, where the services of a probation officer are always available to one or other or both parties. I hope that there may come a time when every County Court has such a welfare service. The hopeless inadequacy of many of the people who come before County Courts make this in my view a highly desirable innovation in County Court procedure. And it needs no legislation or alteration of the law.

*

Over the years I tried a large number of possession cases. I was particularly sorry for the parties when proceedings were brought on the grounds of nuisance or annoyance, just as I was sorry for neighbours who quarrelled. Often in a nuisance case the faults were evenly distributed between landlord and tenant. The parties or their wives hated each other. I did my best on such occasions, if I didn't make a possession order, to try to restore some harmony in the house, but I don't suppose that I was very successful. But one thing I was adamant about. I would not compel a clean landlord to live with a dirty tenant. And so solicitors for landlords knew that, if they could show that as a result of the tenant's habits, the landlord or one of his other tenants had to endure unpleasant smells I should be likely to make an Order for possession if the nuisance were not permanently abated.

In one of these cases I had what I considered to be a mild triumph. A white landlord sought an Order for possession

against a black tenant on the ground of nuisance and annoyance. All sorts of allegations were made against the tenant, but
I was not impressed with any of them until an allegation of
smell was made. I then said that I would come to the house and
inspect the premises myself.

I went there and the door of the tenant's sitting-room was
opened. I looked in. There was the most charming sight before
me. Six little piccaninnies sitting in a row, wide-eyed on a sofa.
But I couldn't look at them for more than a moment, much as
I should have liked to have done so. The smell drove me out.
It was appalling.

We went back to court, and there I said that I found all the
facts in favour of the tenant except that of smell. As far as that
was concerned, I said that, unless the tenant could put an end
to that nuisance within six weeks, he and his family would have
to leave. I advised him to go to a local welfare officer for help
as to how to eliminate the smell. I very much disliked the idea
of turning out a husband and a wife and six little children, yet
it was quite intolerable that other people in the house should
have to put up with such an appalling smell. But, as the tenant
and his wife lived with it, they obviously couldn't smell it themselves, and in those circumstances I didn't really see how they
could put it right. That was why I advised them to seek help.
I made it quite clear that, if ever I went to the premises again
and noticed a bad smell, I should unhesitatingly make a
possession order against the tenant.

I forgot all about the case until a year later when the landlord restored it before me. He made various allegations against
the tenant but not that of smell. This meant that somehow or
other the tenant had managed to cure it, because the landlord
must have known that he was sure to win if the smell had
persisted.

The story has a happy ending, because, although I found in
favour of the tenant, the local authority rehoused the whole
family, so that everyone was satisfied.

*

As a result of the Report of the Withers Payne Committee, judgment summonses have now been abolished. No one is now liable to be sent to prison for failing to pay a civil debt, even though failure is due to some extravagance, e.g. when a person, ordered to pay £2 a week in respect of a debt for a car, spends £2 a week on a television set instead of complying with the Order.

I objected to sending people to prison when they had committed no crime, but it was necessary the Orders of the court should be obeyed. In most cases it was only possible to know what a fair Order for payment by instalments by a debtor would be if the debtor attended and told the court what the situation was. Sometimes the debtor did not attend and he was then ordered to attend on pain of imprisonment. To prevent debtors actually going to prison I instructed bailiffs always to take them to prison via my court. Once he arrived at my court the object was achieved, he could be asked the necessary questions and I would then discharge the Order for imprisonment. This was a new procedure which came into effect some years after I had become a judge. Before the introduction of the new procedure it had been possible simply to arrest the man and to bring him to court, which was all that was necessary. But, because the existence of this power of arrest was a little difficult to ascertain, a good many judges did not use it.

This was the origin of the scene in *Brothers in Law* where Roger Thursby, briefed to cross-examine a debtor about his means, goes to a County Court only to find to his horror that the debtor is not there. The judge asks Roger what he wants him to do and Roger is tongue-tied. An older colleague whispers to him: 'Ask for a 271.' So Roger asks for it.

'What on earth is that?' asks the judge.

The colleague has gone by this time and Roger hasn't the faintest idea what a 271 is and the judge dismisses his application. In point of fact a 271 is a form in the County Court which authorizes a bailiff to arrest a witness and to bring him into court to be examined as to his means. But few judges knew of this and, in consequence, the procedure was changed. If the debtor did not attend, the judge's only power was to send him to prison for fourteen days. That was no earthly use to a creditor and I must say that I thought the change a foolish one. However, it didn't make much difference in my court because, by giving the instructions which I have mentioned, it was not necessary for the debtor to go to prison.

However, after a time I found that some debtors were taking advantage of this and flouting the Orders of the court. So I said that, if the debtor did it twice, I should be forced most reluctantly to send him to prison. But it was quite unnecessary for him to serve the full fourteen days and, when I was satisfied that I had no alternative to sending a man to prison, I would ask him when it would be convenient for him to go. If he went on a Friday afternoon, for example, he would be able to come out on the Monday morning and wouldn't lose any work. Sometimes the actual imprisonment would be postponed for several months, at the debtor's request. I felt sure that for a man who had never been to prison a couple of days there would be quite sufficient to prevent him from flouting the Orders of the court again, and it would show to other debtors what would happen to them if they persisted in disobeying the Orders made against them.

But I am bound to admit that on one occasion when I asked a debtor when it would suit him to go to prison I could not help thinking of the passage in *The Mikado* when the Mikado asks Pooh Bah:

'Now about your execution, will after luncheon suit you?'

*

While I was a judge I had personal experience of the unreliability of honest, independent witnesses of an accident, who have not been concerned in it in any way themselves but have been standing about or walking on the pavement.

I had been sitting in the Divorce Court and had parked my car in one of the car parks at the Law Courts. I wanted to go west along the Strand and accordingly, when the road was clear, I drove across it from the Law Courts and turned right.

I was still in second or third gear when the mate of a lorry-driver came out on foot from one of the side turnings on my left (Surrey Street) and held up his hand for me to stop, because the lorry wanted to back out into the Strand. He did this when I was about the length of a cricket pitch away from him and, as I was going slowly, I had plenty of time in which to stop. I gave the slowing-down signal with my right hand and gradually pulled up to a halt, giving the lorry-driver plenty of room in which to pull out. I had been stationary fully for two or three seconds, it may have been more, when I was suddenly propelled forward from behind. I had been run into by a bus. Either the driver had been going too fast or his brakes were not efficient enough, or possibly it was a bit of both. Before I had time to get out a bystander rushed up to me and said: 'I saw it all, sir. It wasn't your fault at all. I'll give you my name and address if you like.' I said: 'Thank you very much.' He then said: 'It was entirely the fault of the lorry-driver.' I said in some surprise: 'The lorry-driver?' 'Yes, indeed,' he said, 'I saw the way you had to stand on your brakes.' I didn't enquire from the man whether at one time he had been a bus-driver or bus-conductor or in some way concerned with buses, but, unless he had been, there was absolutely no reason why he should give me this entirely false account of the accident. The lorry-driver had behaved perfectly properly by sending out his mate to give the necessary signal to the traffic, his mate had behaved perfectly properly by signalling to me in plenty of time and causing me no inconvenience whatever and I had only had to apply slight pressure to my brakes to come to a standstill. I can only imagine that the bystander had once been inconvenienced by a lorry backing out from a side turning without giving him sufficient warning, but of his honesty I had no doubt. He really thought that the accident had happened as he said.

And then I had a slight, though not unpleasant, shock. I drew my car to the side of the road and got out, and a bus inspector came up to me. He told me that he had seen it all and added that, while he couldn't make any admissions on behalf of the

L.P.T.B., he did not suggest that I was in any way to blame. He then said:

'Aren't you Judge Leon, the judge of the Willesden County Court?'

I said that I was.

'Not so long ago,' he said, 'you decided a possession case in my favour.'

I hope that the next episode will not make readers think that I am accident-prone or that there is something about the back of my car which incites other drivers to give it a bang.

I was stationary in Birdcage Walk when a car ran into me from behind. I got out and went up to the driver, who was an extremely pretty girl.

'I'm terribly sorry,' she said. 'I'm always doing that.'

When I told that story to Nina Bawden she capped it with one of her own.

'I was driving in a long line of traffic,' she told me, 'starting and stopping the whole time. I got fed up with it and started to read. Suddenly I was horrified to find that I had run into a beautiful new car in front. The driver leaped out of his car and came up to me, fuming.

' "I'm terribly sorry," I said, "I was reading."

' "My God!" he said, and went straight back to his car without taking my number.'

I should have thought that insurance companies might give a special rebate on the premiums for pretty girl drivers.

*

Against the many points which can no doubt be made against me as a judge, I should like to claim one point in my favour. For some time before 1965 I had not been satisfied that many of the debtors who went to prison under the law which existed between 1869 and 1971 should have gone there at all. So I obtained permission to investigate the matter.

Judge Mais (now Mr Justice Mais) and I, together with my Registrar Stanley Prothero, went to Brixton and interviewed four debtors. After we had questioned them, the three of us and the Prison Governor were all satisfied that none of the men should have been in prison at all. We had no doubt that, if, when the bailiffs arrived to take them to prison, they had applied to the court to have the Orders for their imprisonment revoked or suspended, any judge would have granted their applications. Their reason for not applying was, as I had suspected, their inadequacy and lack of ability to communicate. In consequence of our visit, Judge Mais and I wrote to the Lord Chancellor's Department, which acted with extreme promptitude. Within a week every County Court had been instructed to take steps to ensure that, before a man went to prison, the right to have the Order revoked or suspended was made clear to him. In consequence of these instructions the imprisonment rate immediately dropped by half and remained at that lower figure. In actual numbers this meant that between 1965 and 1971 (when the law was altered and imprisonment for debt abolished) between five and ten thousand people did not go to prison when otherwise they would have done so. All the same, it is rather horrifying to think that between 1869 and 1965 probably over a hundred thousand people went to prison when they should not have done so. Although I can at least claim the credit for instituting the enquiry, I was appointed a judge in 1949 and I can hardly look with complacency on the fact that it was fifteen years before I did anything about it.

*

I have sometimes been asked if I ever lost my temper on the Bench. If 'not obviously' is a fair answer to this question, it is probably because of my close association with my brother Walter, who has a more agreeable character than I have. He had a very quick temper, which appeared and disappeared in a trice. Never having cared for a shouting-match, my response during our occasional quarrels as small boys was to become as cold as he was hot. I knew that this behaviour would irritate him even more. So, if counsel became annoyed with me, I would become more and more amiable. From the point of view of the public and the dignity of the Bench, this was better than a show of hot temper or sullenness, but it could, I suppose, be called a display of cold temper, and is not a quality to be proud of. I think and hope that there were few occasions when I exhibited this but, when I recall the behaviour of judges like Snagge or Geoffrey Lawrence or many of the others to whom I have referred, if I had regrets, they would be for those occasions.

⚏ The Divorce Court

One part of my duties which I did not like was my obligation to sit in the Divorce Court once a fortnight. During the whole time that I was a judge, there was no divorce by consent and, worse than that, the party who asked for a divorce had to prove that there was no conduct conducing, no connivance, no condonation and no collusion, even though the petition was undefended. Some judges only paid lip-service to these matters and granted a decree in a manner little different from a clerk in the Post Office supplying a stamp. I was too technically minded to do this and created a good deal of alarm and despondency among the Bar by insisting upon trying each case properly, as though it were a real case. I disliked doing this and I would accept almost any excuse for allowing the case to be transferred from my court to a more suitable judge. Three times I applied to the Lord Chancellor to be relieved from doing the work. The third time I was lucky and for my last few years on the Bench I did not do divorce work. I have no doubt that the Bar was extremely grateful.

But one practitioner at the Divorce Bar defeated me. This was John Mortimer's father, Clifford Mortimer, Q.C., about whom his son wrote that charming and successful piece for the theatre, *Voyage Round my Father*. Mr Mortimer did not, however, mention one little ploy of his father's. Mr Mortimer senior had been a very able and experienced member of the Probate and Divorce Bar, but he became totally blind and his health was not good. When he was engaged in an undefended divorce case his wife would lead him to the Bar and he would sit down there, with his brief in Braille in front of him. The case was called on and he would get up slowly and say:

'My Lord, I haven't been very well recently. Would your Lordship allow me to conduct the case sitting down?'

'Certainly, Mr Mortimer. Pray sit down.'

He would then call his client and examine her or him from his Braille brief. How could any human judge ask any of his witnesses or Mr Mortimer himself any question which might show that there was conduct conducing, condonation, connivance or collusion? Here was this poor old man, led into court, perhaps rather like Samson by the Philistines, when he was in failing health and almost at the end of his days: how could one know that this would not be his last case? I am quite sure that every technically minded judge before whom he appeared in such cases prayed that nothing would happen which would compel him to intervene. I know that I did and I don't think that I ever did intervene. But I have no doubt that Mr Mortimer senior was well aware of the power which he was exercising over the court. I said to myself that, if ever a friend of mine had a difficult undefended divorce to come before the courts, I would recommend him to have Mr Clifford Mortimer as his counsel.

One of the things I objected to about the discharge of this jurisdiction was the almost obscene way in which a judge was required to make quite certain that, when adultery was charged, it really had been committed. In some cases it really must have seemed to the parties as if the court wanted to have seen the adultery committed personally. All this has virtually been abolished, now that divorces can be obtained by consent, and I shouldn't in the least have minded sitting in the Divorce Court today.

As a result of my insistence that adultery must be properly proved, cases sometimes had to be adjourned for additional evidence. On one occasion the waiter from some London hotel, where the respondent husband was said to have stayed with a woman not his wife, identified a photograph of the respondent as being the man who had stayed in the particular room at that hotel on the night in question. The waiter had seen him there for about five minutes. Two months later he was shown a photograph of him which he identified and the trial took place nine months later. He unhesitatingly identified the photograph as that of the husband. I asked him how he was able to do this when he'd only seen the man for five minutes. He replied that he had got a particularly good memory for faces. Counsel then handed up another photograph and asked him whether he had ever seen the person in that photograph before. He looked at the photograph carefully and said that he had not. I felt quite sure that this was in fact a photograph of the wife who had given evidence in court before the waiter. She was in the witness-box for about a quarter of an hour. I asked him to look at the photograph again. He did.

I said: 'Are you quite sure you've never seen the person in that photograph before?'

He said he was quite sure.

I then asked him if he was in court when the petitioner gave her evidence and he said that he was. I asked him if he'd looked at her while she was in the witness-box and he said that he had. I then asked for the photograph to be brought to me and it was, as I suspected, a photograph of that woman. He didn't seem to have a very good memory for faces that morning. So the case had to be adjourned for better proof of the adultery. It can be said, and no doubt was said, that I ought to have turned a blind eye to such matters.

I did have one rather curious case. It was a petition by a wife against her husband on the grounds of desertion. As it was so easy for a person to say that her husband or his wife had left the house and stayed away for three years, I always wanted to know what the circumstances were in which they came to live apart. So I asked the wife to give me a detailed description of what happened.

'It was like this,' she said. 'We were playing chess together one evening and in the middle of the game I asked him what he would like for supper, saying that I was proposing to have a

Welsh rarebit. He said he didn't want a Welsh rarebit but he would like a poached egg. I said, "All right", and, when the game was finished, I went and cooked the Welsh rarebit and the poached egg. Apparently the smell of the Welsh rarebit being cooked permeated from the kitchen into the sitting-room where my husband was and, when I came in with the Welsh rarebit and the poached egg, he said that the Welsh rarebit smelled so good he'd have it instead and I could have the poached egg. I said, "No, I offered you the chance of having a Welsh rarebit but you preferred a poached egg and I want a Welsh rarebit." So I gave him the poached egg and I ate the Welsh rarebit and from that moment he never spoke to me again. He left me some days later.'

Today the situation in the Divorce Court (now called 'the Family Division') is quite different. (It seems rather a pity to use the word 'Family' which for most people has happy associations, as the name of the division where families are broken up.) Divorces are granted by consent if there has been separation for a certain length of time. In many of the cases which used to come before the courts there had been separation but it had been separation by consent, and one of the parties had to pretend that he or she had been deserted if the divorce petition was to be successful. It must have been a great temptation, which I suspect was seldom resisted, for a separation by consent to be converted into desertion by one or other of the spouses.

I think that it is a great pity that there are so many divorces. A successful marriage is the foundation of happiness for both parties, but, if the parties simply can't get on together, it is far too late in the history of matrimonial affairs in this country to deny them release from a situation which has become intolerable to both. Being happily married myself and having been happily married twice I deeply sympathize with those who are not. Most of the judges I know are, I believe, happily married and I am sure that this is an advantage to the litigants who appear before them, because a happy and secure judge is likely to be more compassionate and understanding than a lonely or misunderstood one.

❖ Witnesses

One of the things that never ceased to amaze me was the apparent ease with which the majority of witnesses gave evidence. They cannot have been at ease, but most witnesses were in fact able to tell a clear, intelligible tale, which they usually believed to be true. But I knew that in most cases they must have been extremely nervous and far from at ease. As I have said before, after I had been a judge some years, I did the best I could to make their stay as comfortable as possible.

There are, of course, a few witnesses who enjoy going into the witness-box. They are very extrovert people, they like taking the centre of the stage, they hope that the Press will be present and report their evidence and, in effect, they have come to court to enjoy themselves. Such are the people who sometimes give their names to drivers after an accident. They hope that there will be a court case and that they will be summoned to tell their story. They are witnesses to beware of. In many cases they heard a bang and looked up and have no idea what happened. However, by the time they come to court they have seen everything that happened up to the moment of the collision. I don't, of course, mean that independent witnesses of an accident are never reliable, but, if a person has no reason whatever to be watching the vehicles or people concerned in the accident, his evidence, even though honestly given, is often not to be relied upon. Accordingly, where such a witness gave evidence I usually asked him a question or two to see whether he was a professional bystander. On one such occasion I received a surprise.

Judge Edgedale, who was sitting in my court as the second judge, had sent me a note to ask me if I would re-try a case which he had started to try and which, for reasons which he did not disclose, he had had to abandon. This occasionally happens, for example when a judge is accidentally told in the course of a case that a certain sum of money has been paid into court by the defendant. Under the rules a judge is not allowed to know this, in case it affects the amount which he eventually awards (if any). There are, of course, other reasons why a trial may prove abortive, but naturally one does not ask what the reasons are. In this particular case I simply went on to try the case afresh.

It was a claim for damages arising out of a street accident and the plaintiff's case was that the accident was due to a concertina collision. He said that he had been driving in the middle of a main road in a long line of traffic which kept on stopping and starting. On one occasion, after he had been stationary about eight or ten seconds, the defendant's car ran into him from behind. This is a well-known type of accident and usually the defence is that the plaintiff pulled up too sharply or failed to give a signal or something of that kind. Even so it is very rare that some blame is not to be attached to the defendant. The defence in this case was very different. The defendant said that the only true statement which the plaintiff had made was that there was a collision in that road at that time between their respective vehicles, but, he said, it arose in this way.

'Both the plaintiff's vehicle and mine were stationary, parked at the side of the road,' he said. 'The plaintiff's car was in front of mine, and apparently he wanted to move away but was unable to do so because of a car parked in front of him. The accident was caused by his backing into my car.'

The plaintiff said that this was a complete fabrication and I must say that I preferred the way in which his evidence was given to the way in which the defendant gave his evidence. Moreover, the damage seemed to me rather more consistent with a collision caused by a car behind running into the car in front than by the car in front backing into the car behind. However, there was no expert evidence on this matter and a judge has to be extremely careful in cases like this before allowing such a matter to affect his decision one way or the other.

The defendant then called a witness, who said he was standing on the pavement near to the defendant's car, which was stationary by the side of the road when the plaintiff's car, which was parked in front, backed into it, as the defendant had claimed. The witness said that he did not know either the plaintiff or the defendant before the accident. Here, then, appeared to be a truly independent witness whose evidence completely corroborated that of the defendant. At that stage in the case I provisionally came to the conclusion that, although I preferred the plaintiff as a witness, it was for him to prove his case and that on the evidence as it stood at that moment, I could not possibly say that he had proved it. However, as I said, I am a little chary of independent witnesses. So, at the end of his evidence, I said to him:

'Mr So-and-so, have you ever given evidence in a case like this before?'

'Yes,' he said. 'I was involved in a concertina collision myself.'

'I see,' I said. 'But, apart from that case and this, have you ever been in court before in your life?'

The witness seemed to me to be a nice young man of about twenty-eight or thirty. I firmly expected him to say that he had never been in court before and, if he had said that, I should have given judgment for the defendant. In fact, however, he said:

'Need I answer that question?'

'Why don't you want to answer it?' I asked.

'I've got a record,' he said.

'For what?' I asked.

'Oh, burglary and housebreaking.'

'How many convictions?' I asked.

'Oh, about eight.'

His answers showed that I was not a good judge of a witness's appearance. I thought he looked a very decent young man and I hadn't the faintest idea that he had all those convictions against him. Perhaps my eventual decision in the case was wrong, but I can only say that, if you want an independent witness to corroborate you in an accident case, you should choose someone who has not got eight previous convictions for burglary and housebreaking.

But the oddest thing about the case was the reason why Judge Edgedale had transferred the case to me. As soon as the plaintiff and the defendant had given their evidence, he had said:

'I find for the plaintiff.'

Whereupon the defendant said: 'But I've got an independent witness.' Judge Edgedale realized that in those circumstances he could not go on with the case, so he asked me to re-try it. But I learned subsequently that, after the case was over before him, he said to the Registrar:

'I saw his independent witness sitting in the court. Didn't like the look of him at all. A burglar or something.' I said that he was a better judge of character than I was.

*

Some people think that a judge is always able to get at the truth and I have met judges who clearly do think that they can nearly always tell when a witness is speaking the truth. I don't pretend that I can. I judged cases in the main upon the whole of the evidence before me, on all the circumstances of the case and in particular the documents, and upon the probabilities. I thought it very dangerous to rely on hunches that a person was a liar. To begin with, as I have already pointed out, it is an extremely unnerving experience to give evidence in a court of law. A majority of witnesses only do it once. It is very easy for their recollection to fail or for them to make a mistake, or for them to be so harassed by cross-examination that sometimes they hardly know what they are saying.

I remember one witness, who had been a Customs official, giving a fairly bad account of himself in cross-examination. At the end of it I said to him:

'Mr X, as a Customs officer I suppose it was your duty sometimes to ask people questions about their luggage.' He said that it was.

'And I suppose,' I went on, 'they sometimes told you lies in reply to your questions.' He said that was indeed so.

'And in those cases,' I said, 'I expect you asked them further questions.'

'Yes.'

'And sometimes the people concerned lost their heads and said anything to you, true or false.'

'Yes,' he said, and then added: 'Like I'm doing now.'

Another witness gave a rather similar answer in reply to one of my questions. He also had been cross-examined by counsel and had made a bad impression on me. But, realizing that he might not have done himself justice by his answers, I asked him a few questions myself. His answers to me, however, were extremely unsatisfactory. So I said:

'Now, look, Mr So-and-so, if you'd been the judge and I'd been the witness and I'd answered your questions as you've answered mine, what would you have thought?'

'I'd have been a bit dubious, your Honour,' he said.

The witness who tries to be funny seldom is, but unconsciously a witness may be extremely funny. For example, an old man came into the witness-box and it was obvious from the way in which he took the oath that he was extremely deaf. So I said to him in a very loud voice:

'Mr So-and-so, can you hear what I say?'

The old man cupped his hand over his ear and turned to the usher and whispered loudly: 'What's he say, what's he say?'

The usher replied: 'The judge wants to know if you can hear what he says.'

'Oh, perfectly, perfectly,' said the old man.

An old lady was applying to me for more time in which to

leave her house. She had lived there for fifty years and the only reason why the landlords had applied for possession of the house was because it was falling down. She was offered alternative accommodation, as it was dangerous for her to go on living there. But she had lived there for so many years that she was very reluctant to leave it and wanted to stay there as long as possible. She employed a solicitor to appear for her, but even he would not ask me to grant her more time, because he was frightened that, if his application were successful, his client might be killed during the additional period which he had obtained for her. She was a very nice old lady and I told her that I should like to give her more time but that, if I did so and she were killed as a result of the roof falling on her, people would say that it was my fault.

'I'll leave a note behind to say that it wasn't,' she said.

The case has a happy ending because I granted her more time, she was not killed during that period and in due course she was safely rehoused.

In another case a woman said that her husband had been in prison. I asked how long for, and she said that he had just come out after six weeks. He had had his appeal allowed.

'Is it the first time?' I asked.

'It's the first time,' she answered with a broad grin, 'that he's had his appeal allowed.'

I've already spoken about the form of the oath, but some people query whether the taking of an oath makes any difference to the quality of a witness's evidence. On the whole I think that it sometimes does but I only have proof that it did in one case. The question arose as to how a debtor should pay an admitted debt. What were the instalments to be? In such cases it is not always necessary for the debtor to take the oath, because normally his statement about his earnings and outgoings is reasonably accurate. So, without taking the oath, the debtor stated what he was earning and what his liabilities were. For some reason, I suspected that what he was saying was not true. So I asked him to take the oath. After he had been sworn, he said:

'Now I'm on oath, I'll tell the truth.'

And he went back on most of the things he had previously said.

There was another occasion when a man owed money to a hire-purchase company and I had to decide by what instalments he should pay it. In order to come to a decision I naturally had to know how much he was earning. The solicitor for the hire-purchase company asked him that question and he said he was earning £18–£20 a week. The solicitor then asked him if he was earning the same amount as he was earning when he entered into the hire-purchase agreement and he said that he was. The solicitor then handed him a copy of his application to enter into the hire-purchase agreement and asked him whether it was his signature. He said that it was. The solicitor then pointed out that on that application form he said that he was earning £20–£25 a week.

'Well,' said the man, 'your people wouldn't have let me have the car if I'd said I was earning less.'

I then asked him: 'Mr So-and-so, you put down more than you actually earned in order to get the hire-purchase company to let you have the car?'

'Yes,' he said.

'So what you put down was untrue?'

'Yes.'

'Now, you want me to make as small an order as possible, I suppose.'

'Yes.'

'And you've told me that you only earn between £18 and £20 a week. How am I to know that you haven't said that, not because it's true, but in order to dissuade me from making a larger order than I should otherwise have made?'

'I see your Honour's point,' he said.

Coloured witnesses sometimes give their evidence in rather unusual or attractive language. A good example of this was a girl who was applying to have a man sent to prison for breach of an injunction. Counsel cross-examining the girl asked her whether she was not making this application out of revenge, because she herself had been fined £5 for assaulting him. Not surprisingly she denied this.

'Don't you want the judge to send my client to prison?' asked counsel.

And the girl answered immediately: 'Our Bible teaches us when we pray not to tell God what to do. So it will be with the judge.'

One witness came to my court clad only in a tiger-skin. His name was Sutch, known to the public as Screaming Lord Sutch. Before the case came on, my clerk came to me and said that the chief clerk had seen him and told him to go home and get properly dressed, but he had refused. The case was originally in the second judge's list but, in the circumstances, the chief clerk thought that I had better deal with it. So I agreed and the case was duly called on. Mr Sutch came into court in his tiger-skin and I asked him if those were the clothes that he usually wore. He said that they were and so I said that we would get on with the case. It didn't seem to me that, if what he said was true, I should criticize a man because he wore unusual clothes, any more than I would criticize a monk or an Eastern potentate for wearing his normal garb.

Mr Sutch turned out to be an extremely intelligent young man and he behaved very well in the witness-box. Although two reporters had come into court, no doubt in the hope that there would be some sort of controversy about his clothes to report, there was nothing for them on this occasion.

Complaints are often made about the behaviour of the Press but I can only speak from my own experience. They have always behaved very well as far as I was concerned and on one occasion when I was the judge at Windsor I was certainly most grateful to them. I never looked at the papers in a case before it was called on and so I was slightly taken by surprise when the clerk called 'Jill Esmond Olivier' against a defendant whose name I did not know. Now I had met Jill Esmond in 1927 and my first wife and I got to know her sufficiently well to be invited to her wedding to Laurence Olivier. I had lost touch since then, but it was quite obvious that I could not try a case in which somebody

I had once known was concerned. What I normally would have done would have been to ask the counsel or solicitors concerned in the case to come up to the Bench, when I would have explained to them why I could not try the case. But the defendant was unrepresented. So it had to be done openly.

'Mr Tyrie,' I said, addressing Jill Esmond's counsel, 'is not your client the well-known actress?'

'I don't think so,' he replied.

Then Jill Esmond spoke up from the well of the court.

'I am an actress,' she said.

'I'm afraid I shan't be able to try this case,' I said 'I once knew – my wife and I once knew – the plaintiff.'

'It must have been when I was at school,' shouted Jill Esmond.

'No,' I said. 'It was later than that.'

'Oh, it's the wig that does it,' said Jill Esmond.

And then at last her counsel stopped her from intervening. I said that I was sorry that I should not be able to try the case and that it would have to be heard by another judge.

Now this took place at eleven o'clock with plenty of time for the reporters who were present to send up a paragraph to the evening newspapers. I feared that what I would see in the headlines was something like: IT WAS THE WIG THAT DID IT. JUDGE AND ACTRESS FRIEND. But in fact the matter was not reported at all either locally or in the London newspapers. I have always been grateful to the reporters in question.

*

An exception to the rule that a witness is usually nervous is the case of the expert witness. It is often very difficult for counsel to cross-examine successfully a really first-class expert, unless he has been sufficiently and fully briefed in the matter. I had a case once which was concerned with electronics and at my suggestion the parties agreed to apply for an assessor to be appointed to sit with me, so that I might understand what it was all about. Accordingly, a distinguished electronics engineer was appointed and I must admit that without his help I should not have been able to try the case satisfactorily. The plaintiff's counsel was also an expert in electronics, which was a tremendous advantage to the plaintiff. The defendant's counsel was a young man who may have known more about the subject than I did but was certainly not an expert. However, he was a sensible and able young man. During the case he was cross-examining an expert, who was an electronics engineer, when he asked a question to which he got what was from his client's point of view an unsatisfactory answer. His client whispered to him and was obviously suggesting a further question. I then intervened.

'I realize,' I said, 'that it is very difficult for you, Mr Blank, to cross-examine about this matter without being fully instructed. If your opponent has no objection, would you like to have a quarter of an hour's adjournment so that you can take full instructions upon this particular matter?'

The young man accepted the suggestion and a quarter of an hour later was in a position to cross-examine the witness most effectively.

It is very important from the client's point of view that a solicitor who is going to call an expert witness should have interviewed that witness and taken a very careful statement from him. I once tried a case where a man was claiming compensation from his former employers in respect of an injury which he said he sustained while he was employed by them. The facts were simply that, while employed by those employers, he had fallen off a ladder and hurt his back. His injury was diagnosed as a slipped disc, he was treated for it, eventually appeared to get quite better and went back to work. Subsequently he left that employment and went to other employers and, while with them, without any further accident, he became incapacitated by pain in his back. It was diagnosed as a recurrence of the slipped disc due to the original injury and he made a claim, not against his present employers but against his former employers, in whose employment he was when he fell off the ladder.

They repudiated the claim and the case came before me. Medical evidence was given on behalf of the applicant that he was suffering from a slipped disc and that the strong probability was that this was caused by the original injury. In reply the employers called a well-known orthopaedic surgeon who said that the man was not suffering from a slipped disc at all, that in effect the medical witness for the applicant did not know what he was talking about and that, if they continued to treat the man in the way they were treating him at present, he would never get well. There was too much talk of slipped discs, he said, and this case was a good example.

He then went on to explain in somewhat technical language why he was right and the other medical witness wrong. When he had finished his explanation I said to him:

'Mr So-and-so, whatever it is that this man is suffering from, how do you think he got it?'

'I expect when he fell off the ladder,' he said.

That, of course, was the end of the case, but I suspect that if there had been more communication between the solicitors for the employers and the orthopaedic surgeon, the employers would have been saved a lot of money. I still cannot think what the orthopaedic surgeon thought he had come to give evidence about.

*

I once asked a witness in an ordinary accident case whether he had ever been to the Whitechapel Art Gallery. The driver of a van said that he had left his van in a cul-de-sac by a shop and delivered some bread. When he came back, he said, the rear of his van was damaged and another vehicle which had been on the other side of the road was no longer there. He suspected that that vehicle had caused the damage and the next day he waited for the driver to arrive and he challenged him with running into his van. The driver denied it. He then examined the van and found that there were marks coincident with the marks on his van, and the driver was unable to give any explanation for them. But he repudiated liability and eventually a claim was made against him. When he came to give evidence he said that he had backed his van in order to get out of the cul-de-sac. I asked him whether in backing his van he had struck the plaintiff's van. He said: 'I don't think so.'

I then said: 'Have you ever been to the Whitechapel Art Gallery?' to which he replied at once: 'No.'

The object of the question was to see whether, when he knew that he had not done something, he answered with a simple negative or with the more guarded answer: 'I don't think so.'

The plaintiff's case was a thin one but, having regard to the unexplained marks on the two vehicles and the way in which the defendant gave his evidence, I was provisionally satisfied that the probability was that the plaintiff was in the right. However, the defendant asked for an adjournment in order to give some explanation for the marks on his vehicle. I granted the adjournment but the case never came before me again, because in the interim the defendant admitted liability.

One of the most difficult tasks of a High Court judge is to award damages in an injury case. No amount of money can compensate a man for losing an arm, but some people would be more adversely affected by such a loss from a financial point of view than others. A violinist, for example. Judges in County Courts do not have that difficulty because the maximum amount which can ordinarily be awarded in the County Court is at present £1000. But one of the most curious claims was an action for damages, heard not by me but my brother Walter who had become a County Court Registrar. He tried a small case in which a cinema box-office cashier was suing for loss of wages due to an accident. Having claimed the loss of her actual salary, she went on to claim an amount which she called 'perks'. My brother naturally asked her how it was possible for anyone in her position to get 'perks'.

'We sometimes get "blue" films,' she said, 'and some people who attend these performances do not like to remain in the vestibule for a second longer than is absolutely necessary. They don't want a friend or acquaintance to see them there. So, if they haven't got the exact money for a ticket, they put down a pound, take the ticket and don't wait for the change. They go in so quickly that there's no time for me to call them back and, indeed, they don't want to be called back. This money is put in an envelope and retained for six weeks and, if nobody claims it within that period, the cashier who has taken the money keeps it.'

*

A man who is in the right would in a perfect system of justice always win his case but no country has, or can have, such a system. Courts are manned by human beings and, therefore, mistakes are bound to be made. I remember a litigant in person making some application to me in a case which was going to be tried before another judge. He was one of those litigants who talk rather a lot, but he was quite intelligent. During the course of the argument I said that the judge who tried the case might come to a certain conclusion on one particular matter. To which he replied:

'If he does that, it won't be justice.'

I said: 'Whoever told you that you'd get justice here?'

There are many litigants to whom I would not have made this remark, but I wanted to force him to use his mind.

'But I thought –' he began.

'I know,' I said, 'you thought that you'd come to a court of justice.'

'Precisely,' he said.

'Well, you have,' I replied, 'but it's a court of human justice, we cannot look into the hearts and minds of men and we may believe someone who is not telling the truth and vice versa.'

'But aren't you trained to get it right?' he asked.

'We do our best,' I said. 'But how can we always be sure that we are right in our estimation of a witness's evidence? It must be an extremely difficult thing to give evidence in the courts, particularly for someone who has never been in such a place before. An innocent person may betray most of the signs of guilt. What innocent husband has never on occasion blushed when asked by his wife if he has been out with another woman, although in fact he hasn't? When a witness is subjected to examination and cross-examination and questioning by the judge, he must feel sometimes that he is suspected of not telling the truth and, if he does feel this, in many cases it may detrimentally affect his manner of answering.'

'I hadn't thought of that,' he said.

'So you see, Mr So-and-so,' I went on, 'now that you realize the difficulties, you may be able to appreciate that I cannot guarantee that the judge who tries this case will decide in your favour, even if you are in the right.'

'I'm glad you told me this,' he said. 'I thought the courts of this country were always right. There isn't much point in going before them if they aren't.'

'Don't be too apprehensive,' I said. 'Most cases *are* decided correctly, but there must be a number which are not. I hope that yours will be one of the majority.'

I'm afraid that he lost his case, but whether or not he was in the right I shall never know.

◫ Changes in the Law

It may be of interest to consider what are the most important changes which have taken place in the law since I was called to the Bar in 1923.

How important a change is to a particular person depends upon his point of view. For example, there is no doubt whatever that the most important change, from the point of view of the legal profession and in particular from the point of view of the Bar, was the Legal Aid and Advice Act 1949, the result of which, coupled with the increase in crime, I have already mentioned. I wonder if any deeply religious member of the Bar would be prepared to pray for a decrease in the crime rate. If he were at the Chancery Bar, he might possibly be able to do so.

For the general public the National Health Acts starting in 1946 have probably been the most important.

For the theatrical profession the removal of censorship from the hands of the Lord Chamberlain (Theatres Act 1968) was very important.

From the point of view of a bookmaker and those members of the public who indulge a great deal in betting, the most important change in the law has been the legalization of betting shops and ready-money betting on pools (Pool Betting Act 1954, Betting and Gaming Act 1960 and subsequent Acts on the same subject). But a bookmaker may be a husband (or, less often, a wife) and from the point of view of married couples I suppose that the most important change has been the Divorce

Reform Act of 1969. Divorce by consent is undoubtedly one of the most important changes in the law. But a bookmaker may not only be a husband, he may be a tenant and the landlord and tenant legislation in the last fifty years (starting with the Landlord and Tenant Act 1927) has been extremely important from the point of view of the tenant. The right to new leases of business premises or compensation for giving them up has made an enormous difference to landlords and tenants.

But a bookmaker who is a husband and a tenant may also want to adopt a child and it is only since 1926 (Adoption Act 1926) that he can obtain an adoption order from the court. And if this bookmaker who is a husband and a tenant and is about to adopt a child is knocked down in the street through the combined fault of himself and the motorist, it is only since 1945 (Law Reform [Contributory Negligence] Act 1945) that he can nevertheless claim damages from the motorist who knocked him down.

And if this bookmaker who is a husband and a tenant, who has adopted a child and has also been knocked down in the street employs a staff on his premises and one member of the staff injures another in the course of his duties, it is only since 1948 (Law Reform [Personal Injuries] Act 1948) that the bookmaker would not be able to rely upon the doctrine of common employment. And if this bookmaker, who has been knocked down in the street, and is a husband, a tenant, an adopter and an employer, is also a consenting adult, it is only since the Sexual Offences Act 1967 that he can consent without being guilty of a crime.

And it is only since 1934 (Law Reform [Miscellaneous Provisions] Act 1934) that, if this bookmaker/husband/tenant/adopter/employer/consenting adult and victim of an accident finds out that the man who knocked him down has died, he can take proceedings against the dead man's estate.

And should this bookmaker with all these other qualifications himself die after 1938 and cut his loyal little wife out of his will and leave all his money to his mistress, his loyal little widow will be entitled (Inheritance [Family Provisions] Act 1938) to ask the court in effect to overrule the will and to grant her such provision out of the estate as the court thinks fit. And should the loyal little widow, in spite of the provisions made by the court, get into financial difficulties and incur debts which she does not pay, since the Attachment of Earnings Act 1971 she will no longer be liable to be sent to prison, even if she hired a television set at £2 a week instead of paying £2 a week to her creditors.

These are perhaps some of the more important alterations which have taken place in the substantive law of the country. There are, of course, others, such as the right to take proceedings against the Crown (Crown Proceedings Act 1947) and the release of a husband from liability for his wife's torts (Law Reform [Married Women and Tortfeasors] Act 1935), while Lord Birkenhead's Law of Property Act 1925 completely reorganized the law about real property. The most important alteration from the point of view of legal administration is the Courts Act 1971, and the Act which enables those charged with crime to be committed for trial far more expeditiously (Criminal Justice Act 1967).

I should also refer to the decision of *Rondel* v. *Worsley* (1969 1 A.C. 191) which has resulted in many members of the Bar insuring against possible liability for negligence.

On the criminal side perhaps the most important change from the point of view of violent thugs and writers of thrillers is the abolition of the death penalty.

From the motorists' point of view I suppose that the provisions requiring compulsory Third Party Insurance, which have only existed since 1934 (Road Traffic Act 1934), and the requirement that would-be motorists must take a driving test are two of the most important alterations in the law.

The different forms of sentence which can now be pronounced (which must be a headache to a newly appointed Crown Court judge who has done little criminal work) are important from the criminal's and the public's point of view. Suspended sentences and parole have only come into existence comparatively late in the fifty years with which I am dealing.

For the first time in the history of the criminal law a crime actually called blackmail has been created. Up to the Theft Act 1968 there were various offences of obtaining property by threats, but that Act for the first time created an offence called blackmail (Section 21) which was intended to replace and to fill certain gaps in the offences which had existed up to that date.

In the last ten years Parliament has been extremely busy. In addition to the Acts already mentioned it passed the first Race Relations Act and the important Redundancy Payments Act (both in 1965), it passed four Acts dealing with immigration control and several Acts to protect consumers of goods. It gave a fillip to inflation by passing the Decimal Coinage Act, it enacted vast changes in local government, it facilitated legal abortion by passing the Abortion Act 1967 and it introduced the breathalyser by the Road Safety Act 1967. The age of majority was reduced to 18 in 1969. But in 1961, perhaps realizing the miserable state of affairs which successive governments were going to create for us, Parliament passed the Suicide Act which provided that it should no longer be a crime to attempt to commit suicide.

But it is not only Parliament which can effect changes in the law. In 1974 the House of Lords decided that you cannot be charged with attempted murder if you shoot a corpse thinking it is alive or with attempting to steal if you put your hand in a stranger's pocket only to find that there is nothing there.

I suppose that most of the Acts of Parliament which have been passed are necessary, but I must say that I look with some degree of sadness at the thinness of the volumes of statutes in the earlier part of the century compared with the fatness of those during the period to which I have been referring.

G

⧈ Evidence and the Police

In 1973 Sir Robert Mark, Commissioner of the Metropolitan Police, delivered the Dimbleby Lecture. It was an important speech, and very effectively delivered, and, if I may say so, I agreed with most of it. His reference to the fact that there are a very few criminals in the legal profession is disputed by very few members of the profession, but proof of criminality against a particular member is extremely difficult to achieve without adopting methods which would not be tolerated in this country.

But there is no doubt that a number of highly respectable members of the legal profession, both at the Bar and among solicitors, in what they honestly believe is a desire to protect the innocent, vigorously oppose alterations to the law which would help to convict the guilty. I refer in particular to the way in which they resist the recommendation of the Criminal Law Revision Committee, presided over by Lord Justice Edmund Davies, that the right of silence by suspected criminals should be modified. Although I know personally some of the opponents of this recommendation and am fully aware of their complete bona fides, I cannot help thinking that they are unconsciously motivated by their desire that a lawyer, defending a man on a criminal charge, shall have as many lawful methods of obtaining an acquittal as he can. More lawyers are concerned with defending than with prosecuting, and successful defences are likely to add to such lawyers' reputations and increase their incomes.

Most people in this country are unnaturally honest. Unnaturally, because in his natural state a man will take whatever he wants if he thinks he can get away with it. Only the fear of injury or retaliation will deter him. But in what we call civilized conditions most people are prepared to forgo their natural inclinations in exchange for the protection which a civilized community gives them from being robbed or assaulted or otherwise ill-treated. This protection has of late become less owing to the increase in crime and the shortage of police. But few people, if any, have become dishonest because of the increased danger of being 'mugged'. Shoplifters carry on their practices, usually because of greed, though very occasionally because of some compulsive urge. But no one has yet given the excuse, when caught, that he did it because someone burgled his house and was not sent to prison.

The average citizen has, therefore, a clear conscience (except in some cases as the result of cheating in a small way the Customs, the Revenue or other public authorities) and he wants to see brought to justice offenders against the criminal law, except those guilty of the minor crimes which he commits himself. But people generally draw a distinct line between cheating the public authorities of a few pounds and stealing anything at all from anybody. Mr A, who would boast of 'getting away with' a small fraud on the Revenue, would not dream of stealing a newspaper from a newsvendor or a toothbrush from a supermarket. And he wants people who do steal caught and sentenced and even more does he want to see removed from society those who are guilty of more serious crimes.

The odd thing is that the average man, although wanting to see crime detected, would deprive the police of one of the easiest ways of proving the guilt of an offender. There appears to be an irrational feeling among many people, particularly among the more intelligent, that guilt must be established without any help from the offender. 'Can you prove it?' asks the offender, and the majority of the public agree with him. It is very difficult to understand why some otherwise intelligent Englishmen have a rooted objection to a man suspected of a crime being asked if he has committed it or being questioned about his movements or behaviour. Everyone would agree that such questions should be asked without the threat of violence or other intimidation, but, provided they are asked properly, what is the objection? If it is thought that you have stolen something why shouldn't you be asked about it? Why should a policeman have to warn you in certain circumstances that you needn't answer?

In the report of the Criminal Law Revision Committee to which I have referred, the well-known comment by Bentham about the right of silence was mentioned. Bentham wrote:

If all criminals of every class had assembled, and framed a system after their own wishes, is not this rule the very first which they would have established for their security? Innocence never takes advantage of it. Innocence claims the right of speaking, as guilt invokes the privilege of silence.

Before referring to this quotation the Report states:

Some lawyers seem to think that . . . it is . . . unfair that a person should be obliged to choose between telling a lie and incriminating himself.

This is the nub of the matter. Many laymen and several lawyers think that no one is liable to incriminate himself. Why on earth not, provided he is not induced to do so by threats or bribes? The Report continues:

There seems to us nothing wrong in principle in allowing an adverse inference to be drawn against a person at his trial if he delays mentioning his defence until the trial and shows no good reason for the delay.

The Committee recommended accordingly, but both the Bar Council and the Law Society spoke out against this recommendation.

But, even if the recommendation of the Criminal Law Revision Committee were accepted, there would still remain the problem of 'verbals', i.e. statements alleged by the police to have been made by a suspect and not reduced into writing. It is very easy for an over zealous or dishonest policeman to invent a confession, but it is equally easy for a criminal to say that he has never made one when in fact he has. The Criminal Law Revision Committee considered this problem, but they made no positive recommendation in regard to it. But there is a solution to that problem which, if adopted, would also solve a far more serious problem – the frequent illegal 'detention of people for questioning' by the police. Unless something is done about this latter problem, one day there is likely to be a public scandal, the result of which will probably be to prevent the police from adopting this procedure in the future. It is highly undesirable that the present illegal police practice should be allowed to continue, but, on the other hand, if the police were given no alternative legitimate power, the result would simply be that many of the criminals who are now caught would go free. Would it not be better to consider adopting the following solution to both problems?

At any time of day or night a police officer, who reasonably suspected that a person might be able to give him information about a crime, should be entitled to take him before a Justice of the Peace and questioned immediately. Once before the Justice, a person would be liable to answer any questions asked him by the police or by the Justice and, if he refused to answer any question, his refusal could be given in evidence if he were subsequently tried for any offence. There would have to be a rota of J.P.s, including those on the supplementary list, so that immediate questioning could be undertaken. The important thing is that, if the police had to wait for several hours before questioning a suspect, he might think up a false excuse or arrange with a friend to give him a false alibi. Tape-recordings should be used so that there could be no question of the evidence being taken down inaccurately or unfairly.

It should further be provided that nothing said by a person accused of a crime, except for the purpose of committing it or in the course of committing it or during the hue and cry after it, should be admissible in evidence unless it was said before a Justice of the Peace. This would do away with any possibility of confessions being said to have been extorted from people accused of crime. It would also do away with the illegal detention for questioning and at the same time give the police a legal method of trying to ascertain the truth about a crime.

No doubt, if the law were changed in this way, there would be an outcry by those who seem to value the right of the suspected criminal to be free from the unpleasantness of being questioned more than the right of the law-abiding citizen to be free from the unpleasantness of being attacked in an underground subway or a London street.

▨ The Next Fifty Years

I enjoyed my first fifty years in the law tremendously, but I am
not pessimistic enough to think that I shall live to complete my
second. My reluctance is partly due to a disinclination, which
I share with most people, to go on living when my mental
powers are substantially reduced, but it is also because I do not
relish the probable alterations in the legal system which I fear
will take place.

Until the Courts Act 1971 there has been little serious change
in the system of the law since the Judicature Act 1873. But the
1971 Act has made some important alterations, of which the
most significant may be the increase in the number of judges.
It is possible that, as a lawyer, I am too concerned about the
importance of the integrity of the legal profession, but I don't
think I am. A legal profession which commands universal
respect must be a great advantage to any country. And as with
battalions in the Army, so with any organization. The standard
comes from the top. I have already expressed the hope that the
trial of liability in road accident cases should cease to take up
the time of the courts, and, should this happen, a brake can be
put upon the speed with which additional judges are being
created. The record of the English judiciary for integrity is
unrivalled in world history, and one only has to look at the
sorry state of the United States of America in this respect to
appreciate how lucky we are.

I fear that within the next fifty years the Inns of Court will disappear. If our legislators should effect this change it will be because they do not appreciate the extent to which the integrity of the profession stems from the close association of members of the Bar and judges in the Inns of Court. This association is vital to the maintenance of the present high standard.

I believe, too, that within the next fifty years the professions of barrister and solicitor will be fused, and that there will simply be twenty-five thousand lawyers. At the moment High Court judges are only appointed from the Bar. There are about three thousand barristers and of those only five to ten per cent are of the right age, ability and experience to be considered for such an appointment. All of the two hundred possible candidates are well known to many people in the profession, and the Lord Chancellor has no difficulty in assuring himself that any person whom he appoints to be a judge is in the highest degree likely to maintain present judicial traditions. But how can there be any certainty that, if a judge is chosen out of twenty-five thousand lawyers, he will be a person of integrity? It will only require one public scandal about a judge to set us back two or three hundred years.

As for the trial of cases in the future, I am not so much worried about the probable use of the computer. After all, the computer can only give out what has gone into it and human beings will always have to feed it. It could even, I suppose, be argued that in civil cases judges could make good use of it. Such cases only have to be decided on a balance of probabilities. If, therefore, a judge fed all the facts of the case into a computer, it should be able to state what the probable result of the case would be. It is true that one judge would decide a case in one way, and that, where it is a borderline matter, another judge might decide it in a different way. But, as the law only requires the court to decide what is the more probable, the computer would be just as likely to be right as the view of either judge.

It would, however, be going too far to arrange for computers to take over in criminal cases. But it would certainly simplify matters if it did. A policeman would take a suspected person to the official computer and feed all the facts into it. The computer would then say what were the chances of an acquittal or conviction. If it said, for example, that the chances were five to one against acquittal, the policeman would produce six cards from which the man would be given the opportunity of choosing one. Five would have guilty written on them and one not guilty. If he drew the right one, he would go free, and vice versa. Such a system would save the time of magistrates, judges and juries. But I don't think that computerization is ever likely to go as far as that, nor would the legal profession be very pleased if it did.

One reform which I venture to suggest ought to have taken place long ago and ought to take place in the immediate future is that all judges should be competent at some form of shorthand. They should be able to take down the evidence at something approaching dictation speed. At present many trials are considerably slowed down by the fact that the judge is taking down the evidence in laborious longhand. This not only wastes time but it sometimes prevents the satisfactory flow of a witness's evidence.

I suppose that no one has so much power in his own province as a judge sitting in court. He can criticize anyone and, even if he does so unfairly, the person criticized cannot answer back without his permission. If anyone persists in disobeying a judge's order to keep silent, he can be sent to prison or fined. The possession of such power requires a deep sense of responsibility. I doubt if any judge in the last hundred years has abused this power by sending anyone to prison unjustly. On the other hand, there have been occasions – not many but one is too many – when judges *have* abused their power by criticizing someone unfairly. A good example was provided by Lord Hewart when he said to a prisoner who had been acquitted: 'You are discharged. You are very lucky in your jury.'

From time to time judges have criticized the advocates or the solicitors in a case and later on have had to withdraw, when the full facts were made known. It is highly undesirable that this sort of thing should happen. It is so easy for a judge to hurt the feelings of a witness or an advocate or of the usher and he ought always to be on guard against saying anything that may have this effect.

As far as I can remember, I have only once exacted a penalty for contempt in the face of the court. A landlord was taking proceedings against a tenant for possession on the ground that she was a nuisance and an annoyance to adjoining occupiers. She was an old lady and I am afraid that she had reached an age when she was unable to control her words or actions. Her neighbours had appealed to the landlords to get her out and, when eventually he agreed to try to do so, they all attended the court to hear the old lady turned out. They sat in serried ranks at the back of the court. The landlord was represented by solicitors and counsel and the old lady represented herself. When it became her turn to say something, she had hardly said a few words when there came sounds of derision from the back of the court and the usher said: 'Silence.' It happened again and he called for silence again. When it happened a third time I said: 'If anybody makes any more noise at all while this witness is giving evidence, I will deal with him or her for contempt of court.' There was silence after that for about five minutes, then the old lady said something and there was a solitary sound of derision from the back of the court.

I said: 'Who did that?' and the old lady pointed at a man.

He got up and said: 'I only coughed.'

If he had denied having made the noise, there was nothing I could have done about it, because I did not know who was responsible and I could not have decided between the two of them. But it certainly was not a cough and he had admitted making the noise, so I said: 'Will you come forward, please?' And the man came forward.

I said: 'You are fined half a crown for contempt of court.'

He said: 'I've only got two shillings.'

I said: 'All right. We'll take that.'

I enjoyed my years at Willesden. If a court through which so much unhappiness and tension passes can be called happy, I think that Willesden County Court could be so called. The staff were splendidly helpful and Mr Price, who was my usher for the whole time while I was there, was a small man in stature but a tower of strength to me. Later he was joined by a man of the same calibre, Mr Tritton. I cannot speak too highly of the kindness and loyalty of these two men. And Mr Price on one occasion produced a gem. When I arrived at court he said he was sorry that my usual clerk would not be able to sit with me because he had to go to the dentist.

'Nothing serious, I hope,' I said.

'Oh no, your Honour,' said Mr Price, 'just something to do with his teeth.'

I was most grateful to my Registrars. First there was Richard Orange whose mind and methods were as tidy as mine were not. He was as meticulous as Hill Kelly and as charming as Snagge. It was a great blow when he died.

Then there was Stanley Prothero, a most able man and a cheerful companion, full of compassion and enthusiasm, which he now displays at Westminster County Court.

I do not miss the work at Willesden, but I do miss my friends there, and it's a very great pleasure when occasionally we have a reunion.

*

I retired from the Bench on my sixty-fifth birthday, when I had sat for eighteen years as a judge. Since retirement I have still remained in the law to some extent. I sat for three years on the Committee which has considered and reported on the law of defamation under the wise and friendly chairmanship of Mr Justice Faulks. I also act as legal adviser on a B.B.C. programme called *Your Verdict*. This is a programme which is now broadcast only on the World Service. A panel of four non-lawyers from different countries express their views about a fictitious set of facts, which they have listened to in the form of a play. I then state what I think the law to be and sometimes what I think of the opinions expressed by the panel. I am nearly always surprised at the ability of its members to express coherent views immediately after hearing the problem. And I greatly admire the apparent ease with which the originator of the programme, John P. Wynn, who is not a lawyer, continues to provide suitable and interesting topics for discussion. His fertility in ideas appears unending. The genial and efficient handling of the programme by the producer, Trafford Whitelock, must be infectious because all who take part in it seem to enjoy themselves enormously. I certainly do.

The chairman who introduces the programme and questions the panel is Roy Plomley, the originator of that famous radio programme *Desert Island Discs*. He invented that programme over thirty years ago and has been appearing in it ever since. There must be few people who have not listened to it at some time and I have always been struck by the gentle and effective way in which he manages to bring out the character of the castaway in only half an hour. It is a natural gift, as Roy Plomley is just as modest and friendly to meet off the programme as he appears on it.

Once I was the castaway myself and these are the records which I choose.

1. Beethoven's Quartet in B flat, Op. 130
2. Beethoven's Violin and Piano Sonata No. 8
3. Bach's Art of Fugue
4. Bach's Double Violin Concerto in D
5. Shostakovich's Piano Quintet, Op. 57
6. A Wiegenlied of Mozart sung by Elizabeth Schumann
7. Dylan Thomas's *Under Milk Wood*
8. Julian Slade's 'Look at me, I'm dancing' from *Salad Days*.

The book I chose was Fowler's *Modern English Usage*, which is a never-ending source of instruction and pleasure. The luxury was a large bottle of aspirin, which, to my surprise, no one had ever chosen before. Aspirin is a most useful drug to have on hand, and, if things had become too much for me, it could have been my means of escape.

Anyone looking at the records which I chose might think that I was brought up to like classical music. But this is not the case. Undoubtedly my parents were fond of it themselves and, while I was under the age of consent (and for rather longer), I played the violin – very badly. I gave it up before I was called to the Bar and I did not become interested in music until about ten years later. I had given my parents an autoradiogram as a present and with it I gave them two symphonies of Beethoven. I heard them played the first time without much enthusiasm and, although it is difficult to believe now, I know that I heard nothing tuneful in either. However, after I had heard them half a dozen times or more, I began to hear a tune and became interested. I enquired if Beethoven had written any more symphonies.

The key to the enjoyment of music by the average person is tune and, although the tunes in much classical music are more difficult to assimilate at first hearing, once the ear is accustomed to overcoming this difficulty there are enough glorious tunes to last one a lifetime. It took me about three months to accustom my ear to pick out the tunes in classical music, and after that I couldn't resist buying records by the dozen. Lettice became equally keen and we acquired a vast library of records. They were, of course, 78s and I have since had to dispose of the lot through lack of anywhere to keep them.

Some little time after I had appeared on *Desert Island Discs* I was asked by the B.B.C. if I would do a radio programme called *Off the Record*. This was a half-hour programme in which I was to talk about music and illustrate my talk with seven records. I talked on tune, pointing out what tremendous pleasure there was in store for anyone who had not yet acquired the ability to listen with pleasure to classical music. The first record I played was another song from *Salad Days*, 'I Sit in the Sun'. There must be few people who don't think that that is a lovely tune and I had it played in the hope that the average listener would agree with me on this matter. Having established what was a good tune, I then took two excerpts from *The Messiah*, 'Oh thou that tellest good tidings to Zion' and 'I know that my Redeemer liveth'. The other records which I had played were Beethoven's Violin Concerto, 'Land of Hope and Glory', Beethoven's Fourth Symphony and, once again, Bach's

Double Violin Concerto in D. I wondered if any listener took to classical music in consequence of my broadcast.

*

Although I believe that tune is the key to the enjoyment of music for anyone who is not tone-deaf, there is no key that I can find to the enjoyment of looking at pictures. When I was twenty-five I arranged to take a girl friend to the Tate Gallery. A few days before our visit she told me that she had never been there before. I expressed suitable horror at her lack of education and she appeared suitably ashamed. On the appointed day we started off. We lost our way. It was my first visit too.

It was not in fact until I was about fifty that I acquired a liking for pictures. As a small boy I had been taken unwillingly round galleries and I had on occasion visited them when I was grown-up. But they gave me no pleasure whatever. Lettice drew and painted very well and I loved her pictures. But that was because of her. During her lifetime I took no interest in art generally. It was only after she died that, in an effort to occupy my mind as much as possible, I tried to acquire a liking for pictures.

It took me about two years before I had reached the position where I would go to look at pictures in a gallery because I wanted to and not because I thought I ought to do so. Even now I think that about half my enjoyment is derived from conceit. I get pleasure from being able to recognize the work of one artist and from being able to differentiate it from that of another. But I do get aesthetic pleasure too, though it was infinitely harder to acquire than my love of music.

I started off by talking to friends of mine, pointing out to them that I was not colour-blind, that I had become extremely fond of music and that I had found tune the key to obtaining this pleasure. What was the key to liking pictures? Frank (Soskice), one of whose ancestors was Ford Madox Brown and who has artistry in his blood, said, 'Open your eyes and look'. But this was no help to me, any more than it would have been any help if, when I was trying to get to like music, someone had said to me, 'Open your ears and listen', unless he had added 'listen for the tune'. When I open my eyes and look at a picture what am I to look for? Is it subject-matter, composition, colour or what? It was easy enough for Frank who had an innate love of pictures and other beautiful things to tell me just to look at them, but it was insufficient for me. So I went round asking other people and was given various pieces of advice, none of which, I am afraid, was of any assistance.

Then one day I went to a cocktail party and there I met Maurice Collis, the author and art critic. I told him my problem and he suggested that I should go to one of the galleries and listen to some of the lectures. I felt instinctively that this was bad advice. People who are already fond of pictures may certainly get some pleasure and instruction from listening to such lectures. But I did not believe myself that it would be any use to me and later on, when I heard the jargon which some of the lecturers used, I realized that I had been perfectly right. For example, on one occasion I was present when a lecturer took his little group to look at Renoir's *La Loge*. I made a note at the time of his actual words. What he said was this: 'The quality of the paint has such a delicate rococo animation.' Although this may have some meaning to people who know a lot about pictures, I do not believe that many of his listeners understood what he was saying, but nobody asked him what he meant.

After Maurice Collis had given me this advice I left him and talked to other people in the party and I drank a number of dry Martinis. After about half an hour, when I felt that the Martinis had given me sufficient courage and that whatever Maurice Collis was drinking had reduced his powers of resistance, I went up to him again. I reminded him of the problem about which I had consulted him and then asked him whether he would take me personally round one of the galleries and try to help me to get to like looking at pictures. He agreed to do so. He said that he regarded the request as an interesting challenge and that he would consider very carefully how to meet it.

'Here you are,' he said, 'if I may say so, a reasonably intelligent middle-aged man, not colour-blind, very fond of music, anxious to become fond of pictures, but in fact getting no pleasure out of them at all. Now it is up to me to break down your resistance to this form of enjoyment.'

We then arranged that I should take him out to lunch about a fortnight later and that we should go to the National Gallery. When the day came round I found that I was starting a bout of influenza but fortunately or unfortunately I did not know his address or telephone number. So there was nothing I could do except meet him at my club and tell him at once that I had influenza and that, if he would prefer it, we should both go home. He said that he was prepared to take the risk of infection. So we had lunch and went to the National Gallery.

The first picture he showed me was Leonardo's *The Virgin of the Rocks*.

'Well,' he said, 'what do you think of that?'

I had to compel my mind to think something about the picture. Normally it would have meant nothing to me. On this occasion the best that I could do was to say:

'The blue looks to me rather like what a pavement artist would have done, the rocks look to me like what you would expect to find in a photographer's studio and, if that is the infant Jesus, he has a gumboil.'

'What do you think of the faces of the Virgin and the angel?' he asked.

'Oh, very nice,' I said. So we moved on to another picture. We stood in front of each of the pictures which he showed to me for some time, and he did his best on each occasion to see if he could find any aspect of the picture in which he could interest me. He most nearly succeeded when he talked about composition, though I cannot say that I was wildly enthusiastic even about that. The pictures which he showed me were Mantegna's *Agony in the Garden*, Bellini's *Agony in the Garden*, Tintoretto's *Vincenzo Morosini*, Titian's *Christ and the Magdalen*, Rubens' *Chapeau de Paille*, Constable's *Hay-Wain* and Rembrandt's *Saskia as Flora* and *A Woman Bathing*.

As we went through the room where there were some French

Impressionists he said that he would not show me those yet. 'You are not ready for the French pictures,' he said, rather as though he were a benevolent but dissolute uncle starting to teach his nephew some of the lower pleasures in life.

I may add that, years before we were married, Barbara had interested her eleven-year-old son in these 'lower pleasures in life' in the Jeu de Paume in Paris. He has liked pictures ever since and has, indeed, painted quite good ones of his own.

I was most grateful to Maurice Collis for the tremendous trouble which he had obviously taken in order to assist me. But, as I did not feel at all well, he could not have given me my first lesson in worse circumstances and I went home to have 'flu without the slightest feeling that I had achieved anything.

However, I intended to go on trying and, when I was better, I went again to the National Gallery and stood in front of each of the pictures which he had shown me. I tried to remember what he had said about them. On each occasion when I went I hoped that enlightenment would suddenly dawn on me. But it did not. It so happened that, after I had seen these pictures a good number of times, there was an exhibition of the École de Paris at Burlington House. Barbara, whom I had not yet married, came with me. At that exhibition for the first time to my knowledge I saw pictures by such artists as Bonnard, Vuillard and Utrillo. It may have been the contrast between those pictures and the pictures which Maurice Collis had shown to me that almost at once I began to take an interest. From then on I began to get positive pleasure from looking at pictures, and Barbara and I went to many exhibitions together. Although, as I have indicated, she already had some knowledge and liking for pictorial art, it is not unfair to say that, whereas Lettice and I started music together, so Barbara and I started pictures.

*

During some of the next fifty years I hope to continue to listen to music and to look at pictures, but two years ago I took up croquet and I hope to go on playing that for some time.

My introduction to croquet involved me in another two

coincidences. I was introduced to the game by a retired judge, Sir Leonard Stone, who is also the resident bencher in Gray's Inn. We play in Gray's Inn together in all conditions. Admittedly it is nicer to play on a bright summer day, but we have played in rain, in snow and in the dark. At any rate we are keen.

Sir Leonard Stone was in the Army in the first war and was captured at Gallipoli. The British commander in his prison in Turkey was Captain Cochrane, D.S.O., R.N. Captain Cochrane was a descendant of the famous Admiral Lord Cochrane, who became the Earl of Dundonald. I wrote a book about Lord Cochrane. It was not concerned with his mighty exploits at sea but with the darkest period of his wonderful career when he was prosecuted in 1814 for a fraudulent conspiracy. It was alleged that he and others had conspired together to deceive the public into thinking that the war had been won and that Napoleon was dead, with the object of making government securities rise in value, so that some of the conspirators might sell such securities at a profit.

Lord Cochrane was convicted and served a sentence of twelve months' imprisonment. He subsequently received a free pardon. The *Dictionary of National Biography* says that the accusation was false, and other books, including his own, have repeated this. I came across the case when I was investigating complaints against High Court judges. Lord Cochrane's case was heard before Lord Ellenborough, and Lord Cochrane bitterly criticized his behaviour at the trial when he made a complaint against him in the House of Commons. I could not understand the nature of the complaints but, as I found the matter a fascinating one to explore, I decided to investigate it as thoroughly as I could. In the result, I came to the clear conclusion that there was no question whatever of the slightest corruption on the part of Lord Ellenborough, although he had not been entirely fair in the way in which he had conducted the trial. But I am afraid that I also came to the clear conclusion that Lord Cochrane was guilty of the crime with which he was charged.

In consequence of the publication of my book I received an

indignant letter from one of Lord Cochrane's descendants, a young man called Douglas Cochrane. He followed up his letter by paying me the compliment of writing a pamphlet about me. He called it 'The Case of Henry Cecil examined'. I invited him to lunch and we have been firm friends ever since.

And the coincidences? Douglas Cochrane turned out to be the son of Captain Cochrane with whom my friend Sir Leonard Stone was imprisoned in Turkey. And not only that, but Douglas Cochrane also turned out to be the nephew of the late Henry Cecil's widow.

*

I sit on a number of committees dealing with prison reform, hospital welfare and copyright. For a year I was chairman of the Management Committee of the Society of Authors and I am now chairman of the British Copyright Council. I wish that the late Sir Alan Herbert, whom I succeeded as chairman, were still in office. He would have been much more likely to achieve one of my objects and I feel reasonably sure that he would have approved of it.

At the moment, copyright expires, in the case of literary works, fifty years after the death of the writer. I should like to see the period extended indefinitely for the benefit of the country as a whole. An immense fund for British cultural activities could be obtained in this way. Anyone can now present Gilbert and Sullivan operas without paying a penny to the descendants of their creators. Since the end of 1974 any film company may film any of Conrad's works without paying anything to Conrad's estate. How much better it would be if a fund under the control of reputable non-political trustees were created by the extension of copyright for the benefit of the arts generally. The money required to finance public lending right could easily be found in this way.

The suggestion that such an extension would, in the case of theatres, cinemas and concert halls, amount to an indirect tax upon the public will not bear examination. What theatre charges less for putting on a play by Shakespeare than a play of

Noël Coward? What concert-hall charges less for a concert of Bach than a concert of Britten? It can be quite fairly argued that, in the case of books, the continued payment of royalties after the fifty years has expired, would amount to such an indirect tax on the public. It would be the most painless form of taxation because books would not go up in price. They would just not go down. Even that complaint could be fairly met by greatly reducing the royalty payable. It would be no hardship to publishers or the public if a royalty of, say, $2\frac{1}{2}$ per cent were payable after the fifty years has expired.

I learned of this idea from Bob Lusty, who still strongly supports it. He would have it made retrospective. I do not personally agree with this for two reasons. First, I don't think it would be fair to those who had invested money in the production of works of out-of-copyright authors. Secondly, I think that the administrative difficulties would be too great.

There are various methods by which the scheme could be put into force. One would be to create a new body like the Arts Council which would have the responsibility of collecting the royalties and deciding upon their use. A good method of collecting them would, in my view, be to employ literary agents for the purpose. But I don't much mind what method of operation is used, provided that some such scheme is introduced into our legislation.

As far as crime and prison reform is concerned, I think that, whatever view may be taken about the philosophy of punishment, the public must be protected from violent people. Those who by their conduct have shown themselves incapable of restraining their violent impulses, whether the violence is for a sexual object or for the purpose of robbing a bank, should be detained in some secure place indefinitely, unless and until medical science is able to show that they have been cured. But, if people are going to be detained indefinitely, they must be detained in decent conditions. They must have interesting and rewarding work, recreation, entertainment and, if possible, though I realize the great difficulties which are involved in this suggestion, conjugal visits.

*

I read a good deal but only non-fiction, except for the novels of friends of mine or when I re-read works of fiction which I have read in the past.

I am very fond of watching cricket and look at it a good deal on television. I also go to Lord's whenever I can. As a small boy one of my greatest ambitions was to have a right to go into the pavilion. Although eventually I achieved this ambition, it was unfortunately not because my cricket was good enough but simply because enough years had passed since I applied for membership. But I love going there and sometimes, when I do, I carry my mind back to the small boy who was too shy to ask P. F. Warner for his autograph. My eldest brother did it for me, and I still have it.

Edward was quite a good cricketer. Walter (at the age of seventy-four) still plays. On his seventieth birthday I went with him to Lord's when he was going to have a little practice at the nets. After the professional had bowled to him for a little time I couldn't resist taking off my jacket and bowling a few balls myself. They were straighter than either of us had anticipated, but otherwise not very different from my deliveries of fifty years ago.

It will be seen that I have quite enough with which to occupy myself during such portion of the next fifty years as I go on living. I still talk to students at schools, technical colleges and universities. I find nothing like enough time for music, reading, croquet and cricket. Nor do I take as much exercise as my doctor thinks I should. I visit him periodically and he always complains at my weight. On the last occasion I said to him:

'But surely you've got fatter patients than me?'

'Oh yes,' he said. 'My fattest patient died yesterday.'

⊞ Index

215